# Blackstone Outdoor Gas Griddle Cookbook #2023

700 Easy Delicious and Affordable Grill Recipes with Tips & Tricks to Master Your Blackstone Outdoor Gas Griddle

**Richard Patterson**

# Table of Contents

# Introduction

Cooking outdoors has become a beloved tradition for many people, especially during the warmer months of the year. Grilling and barbecuing are popular cooking methods, but there's another option that's gaining popularity: outdoor griddle cooking. A gas griddle is a versatile cooking tool that can cook a variety of foods quickly and easily, and it's perfect for outdoor cooking.

If you're new to outdoor griddle cooking or looking to expand your griddle cooking skills, then you've come to the right place. In this cookbook, we'll be exploring the world of outdoor gas griddle cooking and sharing with you some of the best recipes and techniques to help you make the most of your Blackstone outdoor gas griddle.

## About Blackstone Outdoor Gas Griddles

Blackstone is a well-known brand in the outdoor cooking world, and their gas griddles are some of the best on the market. They come in a variety of sizes and styles to suit your needs, whether you're cooking for a large group or just a few people. Blackstone gas griddles are made with high-quality materials and are built to last, so you can be sure that you're investing in a cooking tool that will serve you well for years to come.

Blackstone gas griddles are designed to be easy to use and maintain. They feature a flat cooking surface that heats up quickly and evenly, so you can cook your food to perfection. The griddles are also easy to clean, thanks to their grease management system that funnels grease away from your food and into a removable grease tray.

Cooking on a Blackstone gas griddle is a fun and delicious way to enjoy the outdoors with friends and family. You can cook a wide range of foods, from breakfast favorites like pancakes and eggs to lunch and dinner staples like burgers, steaks, and stir-fry dishes. With a Blackstone gas griddle, the possibilities are endless.

**What You'll Find in This Cookbook**
In this cookbook, you'll find a wide range of recipes that have been specifically designed for use on a Blackstone outdoor gas griddle. We've included recipes for breakfast, lunch, dinner, and even dessert, so you can enjoy griddle cooking all day long. Here's a quick overview of what you'll find in this cookbook:

**Breakfast Recipes:** Start your day off right with delicious breakfast recipes like classic pancakes, breakfast sandwiches, and even breakfast burritos.

**Lunch Recipes:** For a quick and easy lunch, try our grilled cheese sandwich or Philly cheesesteak recipe. Or, if you're looking for something a little more substantial, try our grilled salmon or teriyaki chicken recipe.

**Dinner Recipes:** From juicy burgers and hot dogs to flavorful steaks and stir-fry dishes, our dinner recipes are sure to impress.

**Side Dishes:** No meal is complete without some tasty sides. We've included recipes for classics like grilled corn on the cob and coleslaw, as well as more unique dishes like grilled watermelon and garlic roasted potatoes.

**Dessert Recipes:** End your meal on a sweet note with our delicious dessert recipes, including s'mores, grilled peaches, and even a grilled banana split.

In addition to recipes, we've also included tips and tricks to help you get the most out of your Blackstone outdoor gas griddle. From how to properly season your griddle to how to clean it after use, we'll walk you through everything you need to know to become a griddle cooking pro.

# Breakfast Recipes

## Breakfast Hash Recipe

Time to prepare: 10 minutes
Time to cook: 30 minutes
Servings: 10
**Ingredients:**

- 2 Bags Frozen Potatoes O'Brien
- 1 Sausage Rope
- 8 Slices Thick Cut Bacon
- 12 Eggs
- 1/2 Red Onion
- Green Onion

**Directions:**

1. Light up your griddle after oiling it.
2. After preheating and lubricating your griddle, drastically reduce the heat.
3. To cook this dish, be sure to have two spatulas and a scraper on available.
4. Before anything else, spread out the frozen potatoes on the griddle so they can start to thaw and brown.
5. Stir the scrambled eggs together in a large mixing dish. About half a cup of water is added to the eggs to make them fluffier.
6. While the potatoes are cooking, chop your bacon, onion, and sausage.
7. At this time, I put my onions to the potatoes on the griddle and pushed the potatoes to the other side of the pan.
8. To make the bacon cook more quickly, put it on the opposite side of the griddle and turn up the heat there.
9. Put the sausage in the pan and cook it over low heat; at this temperature, it will cook fast enough.
10. Let them fry for whatever long it takes for the bacon to become the proper crispness.

11. After transferring the meat into the potato mixture, pour the egg mixture on the other side of the griddle.

12. In order to guarantee that the eggs scramble fast, I whisk them around with one of the spatulas.

13. As soon as the potatoes and meat are almost done, begin combining the eggs.

14. After fully combining them, sprinkle on the cheese and switch off the griddle.

15. I rushed in and whipped up some toast as the cheese was melting.

16. Give and enjoy yourself!

## Oatmeal Pancakes

Time to prepare: 15 minutes
Time to cook: 5 minutes
Servings: 8
**Nutritional Info:** Calories 148, Total Fat 5.7 g, Saturated Fat 1.5 g, Cholesterol 23 mg Sodium 170 mg, Total Carbs 21.5 g, Fiber 1.6 g, Sugar 10.2 g, Protein 3.8 g
**Ingredients:**

- ¾ cup old-fashioned oats
- ¾ cup oat flour
- 1 teaspoon baking powder
- ½ teaspoon salt
- 1 egg
- 1 cup milk
- 2 tablespoons vegetable oil
- 4 tablespoons honey

**Directions:**

1. Turn the outside gas griddle's heat to medium.

2. In a bowl, combine the oats, oat flour, brown sugar, baking soda, spices, and salt.

3. Combine the egg, milk, and oil in a separate bowl by beating everything together.

4. Add the flour mixture to the egg mixture in the bowl and stir until slightly moistened.

5. Lightly grease the griddle.

6. Scoop out approximately 14 cup of the mixture and spread it out evenly on the griddle.

7. Carry out step 7 with the remaining mixture.

8. Fry each pancake for two to three minutes, or until it becomes golden.

9. After flipping, heat for a further one to two minutes, or until golden brown.

10. Serve hot with honey drizzled on top.


## Camping Griddle Breakfast

Time to prepare: 10 minutes
Time to cook: 25 minutes
Servings: 5
**Ingredients:**
- Eggs
- 4 Pounds Gold Potatoes
- 1 Pound Bacon
- 5 Polish sausages
- Cheese
- Minced Garlic
- Salt
- Pepper

**Directions:**
1. You should wash and dry your potatoes.

2. The sausages should be polished, and all of the veggies should be chopped and cut into small pieces.

3. To help prevent food from sticking and to facilitate sautéing, put a little oil or bacon grease on your griddle before heating it up.
4. On your griddle, combine the potatoes, onion, and polish sausage.
5. Adjust the amount of salt and pepper.
6. Cook potatoes until they are soft to the touch.
7. Take out the potatoes, then keep them warm on a plate.
8. After the bacon is cooked to your preference, fry the eggs at the same time (or scrambled eggs)
9. Serve everything simultaneously and enjoy yourself! As a garnish, we used shredded cheese, although sour cream would also work.

## Blackstone Monte Cristo

Time to prepare: 15 minutes
Time to cook: 10 minutes
Servings: 6
**Ingredients:**
- 4 eggs
- 1/3 cup of half and half
- 12 pieces of white bread
- 2 tbsp mayo
- 2 tbsp mustard
- 18 thin slices of swiss or gruyere cheese
- 2 pounds deli thin-sliced ham
- powdered sugar
- raspberry jam

**Directions:**
1. Set your griddle on a low heat setting for preheating.
2. Combine the eggs and half and half in a large shallow bowl and whisk until thoroughly combined.
3. Egg wax should be applied on one side of the bread. Put with the egg side down in a single layer on a baking sheet coated with paper.

4. Spread mayo on one side of each pair of sandwich bread and mustard on the other.

5. Place one piece of cheese on each slice of bread. Divide the ham among the 12 pieces of bread in a uniform layer.

6. Put the remaining 6 7. slices of cheese in each sandwich bread half. (There should be three pieces of cheese on every sandwich.)

8. Connect the sandwich parts to create complete sandwiches.

9. Spread plenty of butter on the griddle and place the sandwiches on it. Using a large spatula, cover and carefully push down.

10. Flip the egg mixture over and brown the other side when the egg mixture has set and the bread has toasted.

11. Take the baked goods out of the oven, top with powdered sugar, and serve with raspberry jam alongside.

## Broccoli Pancakes

Time to prepare: 15 minutes
Time to cook: 10 minutes
Servings: 5
**Nutritional Info:** Calories 167, Total Fat 2.5 g, Saturated Fat 1 g, Cholesterol 44 mg, Sodium 77 mg, Total Carbs 29.5 g, Fiber 1.9 g, Sugar 2.9 g, Protein 6.6 g

**Ingredients:**
- 1 cup broccoli florets
- 1 small onion, chopped roughly
- 1 garlic clove, peeled
- 1 egg
- ½ cup whole milk
- 1 cup all-purpose flour
- 1 teaspoon baking powder
- 5 fresh chives, chopped
- 1 tablespoon fresh chervil, chopped
- Salt and ground black pepper, to taste

**Directions:**
1. Turn the outside gas griddle's heat up to medium-high.

2. Place the broccoli, onion, and garlic in a blender and pulse until the ingredients are well diced.
3. Add the egg, milk, flour, and baking powder, then pulse the mixture at a medium speed until it becomes thick.
4. Place the bowl with the broccoli mixture in it.
5. Add the salt, black pepper, chervil, chives, and mix to incorporate.
6. Lightly grease the griddle.
7. Spread an equal layer of the mixture onto the griddle using approximately 2 teaspoons.
8. Carry out step 8 with the leftover mixture.
9. Pancakes should be cooked for around 3 minutes.
10. Gently rotate the pancakes, then cook them for an additional 2 minutes, or until they are golden brown.
11. Present hot.

## Cauliflower Patties

Time to prepare: 15 minutes
Time to cook: 15 minutes
Serves: 6
**Per Serving**: Calories 155 Fat 10 g, Carbs 11.1 g, Sugar 3.9 g, Protein 8.1 , Cholesterol 60 mg
**Ingredients:**

- 2 eggs
- 1 large head cauliflower, cut into florets
- 1 tablespoon butter
- ½ teaspoon turmeric
- 1 tablespoon nutrition yeast
- ⅔ cup almond flour
- ¼ teaspoon black pepper
- ½ teaspoon salt

**Directions:**
1. Use butter to coat the griddle's frying surface.

2. Switch the four burners to medium heat and crank the knobs.

3. Let the griddle 5 minutes to heat up.

4. Fill a saucepan with cauliflower florets.

5. Cover the cauliflower florets with water. For 8 to 10 minutes, bring to a boil.

7. After thoroughly draining the cauliflower, place it in a food processor and pulse until it resembles rice.

8. Place the bowl that is appropriate with the cauliflower rice.

9. Add the other ingredients for the recipe to the bowl, except the butter, and whisk to blend.

10. Shape the cauliflower mixture into tiny patties and cook them on a hot griddle.

11. Cook until softly golden brown, about 3 to 4 minutes each side.

12. Serve.


## Croque Madame

Time to prepare: 10 minutes

Time to cook: 10 minutes

Servings: 4

**Nutritional Info:** Calories: 538; Sodium: 1019 mg; Dietary Fiber: 2.4 g; Fat: 35.2 g; Carbs: 17.8 g; Protein: 36.9 g

**Ingredients:**
- 1 tbsp butter
- 1 tbsp flour
- 2/3 cup milk
- 4 slices thick-cut bread
- 3 slices black forest ham
- 3 slices gruyere cheese
- Salt and black pepper
- 2 eggs

**Directions:**

1. After whisking just till browned, add the milk. The sauce should be stirred until it thickens. After being taken out of the fire, season.
2. Set your griddle's temperature to medium. Each slice of bread is lavishly covered with bechamel sauce on one side and smeared with butter on the other.
3. Add two slices of ham to each sandwich. On the griddle, place it and cook until golden brown. Put the gruyere cheese there.
4. after turning the sandwiches over.
5. Prepare and serve.

## Johnny Cakes with Bourbon Salted Caramel Sauce

Time to prepare: 10 minutes
Time to cook: 25 minutes
Servings: 4
**Ingredients:**
- 1 cup All-purpose Glour
- 1 cup coarse Cornmeal
- 1 tablespoon Baking Powder
- 2 tablespoons Sugar
- 3 large Eggs
- ¼ cup liquid Bacon fat
- 1 cup Buttermilk
- Bourbon Salted Caramel Sauce:
- ½ cup Bourbon
- ¼ cup Water
- 1 cup granulated Sugar
- 3 tablespoon Unsalted Butter
- 1 cup Heavy Cream
- 1 teaspoon Vanilla Extract
- 2 teaspoons kosher Salt

**Directions:**

1. In a large sauté pan, mix the sugar, water, and bourbon. Stirring periodically, bring to a low simmer over medium-high heat until the bubbles are enormous and the color is a pale amber. Stir until everything has melted and combined fully. In a mixing dish, combine the salt, vanilla essence, and heavy cream.
2. Combine flour, baking powder, and cornmeal.
3. In a another mixing bowl, combine the eggs and bacon grease and whisk to combine.
4. Crack the eggs and add the bacon grease to the bowl containing the flour and cornmeal. evenly mixing 12 cups of buttermilk using a spatula Add extra buttermilk to reach the required consistency.


## Italian Breakfast Lavash

Time to prepare: 5 minutes
Time to cook: 15 minutes
Servings: 4
**Nutritional Info:** Calories 266, Total fat 14g, Protein 33g, Carbs 2g
**Ingredients:**
- 2 Lavash Flat Breads
- ½ lb Prosciutto, deli sliced
- ½ lb Capicola, deli sliced
- ½ lb Genoa Salami, deli sliced thin
- ½ lb Mortadella, deli sliced
- ½ lb Mozzarella, deli sliced
- ½ lb Provolone cheese, deli sliced thin
- 4 Eggs
- Balsamic Glaze
- Cento, hot pepper spread
- 2 c Arugula
- 1 tbsp Extra Virgin Olive Oil
- Salt & Pepper, to taste
- Spray extra light tasting olive oil

**Directions:**

1. Turn the griddle's heat down low.
2. Add extra virgin olive oil and salt and pepper to the arugula before serving.
3. Lightly oil one side of the lavash bread and place it on the griddle.
4. Add provolone cheese, Italian meats, and provolone cheese to the griddle and fry two eggs per lavash to the desired doneness. To serve as a binding agent and hold the sandwich together, place the cheese up against the lavash. On top, apply some hot pepper spread.
5. Take the fried eggs from the griddle and distribute them equally over one  side of the lavash.
6. Add roughly a cup of arugula to each sandwich. Balsamic glaze should be drizzled on top. The lavash may be folded in half to create a sandwich.
7.  Savour it by dividing it into thirds or halves.

## French Toast

Time to prepare: 15 minutes
Time to cook: 6 minutes
Servings: 4
**Nutritional Info:** Calories 198, Total Fat 6.4 g, Saturated Fat 1.6 g, Cholesterol 165 mg, Sodium 268 mg, Total Carbs 28.2 g, Fiber 5.5 g, Sugar 9.6 g, Protein 11 g
**Ingredients:**
- ¼ cup milk
- 4 eggs
- 2 tablespoons sugar
- ½ teaspoon vanilla extract
- 1 teaspoon ground cinnamon
- ¼ teaspoon ground nutmeg
- 8 thick-cut bread slices
- ½ cup fresh strawberries, hulled and sliced

**Directions:**

1. Turn the outside gas griddle's heat down to low.
2. In a small baking dish, mix the milk, eggs, sugar, vanilla essence, cinnamon, and nutmeg.
3. Submerge each piece of bread for 5–10 seconds in the milk mixture.
4. Liberally grease the griddle.
5. After placing the slices on the griddle, fry them for approximately 3 minutes on each side.
6. Place strawberry slices on top before serving.

## Kale Omelet

Time to prepare: 5 minutes
Time to cook: 10 minutes
Servings: 3
**Ingredients:**
- 1 tablespoon of fresh sage, chopped
- 4 eggs
- 1/2 teaspoon of pepper
- 4 cups of kale, chopped
- 1/2 teaspoon of salt
- 1/3 cup of parmesan cheese, grated

**Directions:**
1. Your griddle should be preheated to medium-high heat.
2. Spray cooking spray on the griddle's top.
3. On a hot griddle top, cook the kale for a few minutes, or until it has wilted. Whisk the eggs in a bowl before adding the parmesan, sage, pepper, and
& salt.
4. Pour the egg mixture over the kale and let it simmer for 8 to 10 minutes, or until it is firm. Enjoy your meals as is.


## Breakfast Sandwich with Bacon and Cheese

Time to prepare: 10 minutes
Time to cook: 10 minutes

Servings: 4
**Nutritional Info:** Calories 470, Total fat 21g, Protein 38g, Carbs 10g
**Ingredients:**
- 4 tablespoons of Swiss grated cheese
- 4 round rolls sandwiches
- 4 tablespoons of ketchup
- 2 slices of bacon
- Salt and pepper to taste

**Directions:**
1. Start by removing the tops of the sandwiches. Next, using a spoon, remove the inside of the sandwiches, taking careful not to tear or damage the crust.
2. Spread a tiny quantity of ketchup on each sandwich and top it with a slice of bacon and a tomato. In the meanwhile, preheat your Blackstone Griddle for direct cooking at 400°F. An oven-safe baking pan should be brushed with olive oil.
3. Add salt, pepper, and shredded Swiss cheese to the sandwiches and place them within the pan as evenly as you can.
4. Place the pan on the griddle and cook for about 15 minutes. After finished, remove from the heat and serve straight immediately.


## Turkey Pesto Panini

Time to prepare: 5 minutes
Time to cook: 6 minutes
Servings: 2
**Nutritional Info:** Calories 266, Total fat 14g, Protein 33g, Carbs 2g
**Ingredients:**
- 1 tbsp olive oil
- 3 slices French bread
- 1/2 cup pesto sauce
- 4 slices mozzarella cheese
- 2 cups chopped leftover turkey

- 1 Roma tomato, thinly sliced
- 1 avocado, halved, seeded, peeled, and sliced

**Directions:**

1. Turn the griddle's heat up to medium-high. Put 2 slices on the griddle, olive oil side down.
2. Cover one side of the French bread with 2 tbsp of pesto.
3. To assemble a sandwich, layer one slice of mozzarella on the bottom, followed by slices of turkey, tomatoes, avocado, then a second slice of mozzarella. Repeat with the remaining pieces of bread.
4. Cook for 2. to 3. minutes on each side.
5. Serve hot with your preferred soup or salad.

## Cauliflower Hash Browns

Time to prepare: 10 minutes
Time to cook: 10 minutes
Servings: 6
**Nutritional Info:** Calories: 80; Fat: 5 g; Carbohydrates: 3 g; Sugar: 1 g; Protein: 5 g; Cholesterol: 46 mg

**Ingredients:**

- 1 egg
- 3 cups cauliflower, grated
- 3/4 cup cheddar cheese, shredded
- 1/8 teaspoon pepper
- 1/4 teaspoon garlic powder
- 1/4 teaspoon cayenne pepper
- 1/2 teaspoon salt

**Directions:**

1. Turn the griddle's heat to medium-low.
2. Add all the ingredients to the bowl and well combine.
3. Apply cooking spray to the griddle's top.

4. Form the mixture into 6 hash browns, set on a heated griddle, and cook until golden brown on both sides.
5. Present and savor.

## Spinach Pancakes

Time to prepare: 10 minutes
Time to cook: 10 minutes
Servings: 6
**Nutritional Info:** Calories 266, Total fat 14g, Protein 33g, Carbs 2g
**Ingredients:**
- 4 eggs
- 1 cup coconut milk
- 1/4 cup chia seeds
- 1 cup spinach, chopped
- 1/2 teaspoon black pepper
- 1/2 teaspoon ground nutmeg
- 1 teaspoon baking soda
- 1/2 cup coconut flour
- 1/2 teaspoon salt

**Directions:**
1. In a bowl, mix coconut milk and eggs until foamy.
2. Combine all of the dry ingredients, then whisk in the egg mixture.
3. Add spinach and well mix.
4. Turn the griddle's heat to medium-low.
5. Apply cooking spray to the griddle's top.
6. Spoon three to four tablespoons of batter onto the heated griddle surface to form a pancake.
7. Fry the pancake on both sides until just golden brown.
8. Dish out and savor.

# Burgers Recipes

## Lamb and Cucumber Burger

Time to prepare: 5 minutes
Time to cook: 5 minutes
Servings: 4
**Nutritional Info:** Calories 635; Fat 23.7g; Sodium 616mg; Carbs 11.1g; Fiber 1.6g; Sugar 0.6g; Protein 89g
**Ingredients:**
- 1¼ pounds lean ground lamb
- tablespoon ground cuminutes
- ¼ teaspoon ground cinnamon
- ½ teaspoon salt
- ½ teaspoon freshly ground black pepper
- whole wheat pitas
- ½ medium cucumber, peeled and sliced
- ½ cup Simple Garlic Yogurt Sauce

**Directions:**
1. In a medium mixing bowl, combine the lamb, cumin, cinnamon, salt, and black pepper. Using your hands, shape the beef mixture into four 1-inch -thick patties after forking the spices into the flesh.
2. Place the patties on the griddle and grill for 5 minutes over high heat without turning.
3. Take out the hamburgers and keep them hot by covering them.
4. Add a burger, a few cucumber slices, and a dollop of the yoghurt sauce on each pita.
5. Serve immediately.

## Marinated Portobello Cheese Burgers

Time to prepare: 10 minutes
Time to cook: 10 minutes
Servings: 4

**Nutritional Info:** Calories 254; Fat 14 g; Sodium 496mg; Carbs 24.6g; Fiber 1.6g; Sugar 3.6g; Protein 13g

**Ingredients:**

- 4 Portobello mushroom caps
- 4 slices mozzarella cheese
- 4 buns, like brioche
- For the marinade:
- ¼ cup balsamic vinegar
- 2 tablespoons olive oil
- 1 teaspoon dried basil
- 1 teaspoon dried oregano
- 1 teaspoon garlic powder
- ¼ teaspoon sea salt
- ¼ teaspoon black pepper

**Directions:**

1. In a large mixing basin, whisk the marinade ingredients together. Pour the sauce over the mushroom caps to coat them.

2. Bring the griddle's temperature up to medium-high.

3. Arrange the mushrooms on the grill while reserving the marinade for basting.

4. Cook the meat until done, about 5-8 minutes each side.

5. Frequently brush the meat with the marinade.

6. During the last two minutes of cooking, top with mozzarella cheese.

7. Immediately off the griddle, serve the brioche buns.

## Croque Ham Cheese Burgers

Time to prepare: 10 minutes
Time to cook: 10 minutes
Servings: 2
**Nutritional Info:** Calories 475; Fat 30 g; Sodium 641 mg; Carbs 24.6g; Fiber 3.6g; Sugar 4.1g; Protein 26.1g

## Ingredients:
- 2 tablespoons butter
- 1 tablespoon flour
- ⅔ cup milk
- 2 slices thick cut bread
- 2 slices black forest ham
- 2 slices gruyere cheese
- Salt and black pepper
- 2 eggs
- Béchamel sauce, as you like

## Directions:
1. Melt one tablespoon of butter in a small saucepan over medium heat before incorporating the flour. Add the milk after stirring until just browned.
2. The sauce should be stirred continuously until it thickens. Add salt and pepper as soon as you remove the meal from the burner.
3. Medium heat on the griddle
4. Béchamel sauce should be liberally spread on the opposite side of each slice of bread, with one side butter-buttered.
 Heat .
 1. Top each sandwich with the last slice of bread, two slices of ham, and two pieces of cheese. On the griddle, cook the pancakes until golden brown.
2. Top the sandwiches with gruyere cheese, then turn them over.
3. On the opposite side of the griddle, crack the eggs, and cook them until the whites are set.
4. Continue to cook the sandwich until the gruyere on top has melted and the other side is well browned. Each sandwich should have a fried egg on top before being served.


## Beef and Corn Burgers
Time to prepare: 20 minutes

Time to cook: 30 minutes

Servings: 6

**Nutritional Info:** Calories 266, Total fat 14g, Protein 33g, Carbs 2g

**Ingredients:**

- 1 large egg, lightly beaten
- 1 cup whole kernel corn, cooked
- ½ cup bread crumbs
- 2 tablespoons shallots, minced
- 1 teaspoon Worcestershire sauce
- 2 pounds ground beef
- 1 teaspoon salt
- ½ teaspoon pepper
- ½ teaspoon ground sage

**Directions:**

1. In a mixing bowl, combine the egg, corn, bread crumbs, shallots, and Worcestershire sauce.

2. In a another dish, combine the remaining ingredients with the ground meat.

3. Spread waxed paper over a flat surface.

4. Form 12 small hamburger patties from the meat mixture.

5. Spoon the corn mixture equally into the center of each of the six patties, filling it to within an inch of the edge.

6. Place a second circle of meat on top of each burger and press the sides together to seal the corn mixture in the centre.

7. Grill over medium heat for 12 to 15 minutes on each side, or until juices flow clear and thermometer registers 160°F.


## Bulgur Beet Burgers

Time to prepare: 5 minutes

Time to cook: 10 minutes

Servings: 6

**Nutritional Info:** Calories 266, Total fat 14g, Protein 33g, Carbs 2g

**Ingredients:**
- 1 pound beets, peeled and grated (about 2 cups) ½ cup packed pitted dates, broken into pieces ½ cup almonds
- 1 teaspoon ginger powder
- ½ cup bulgur
- Salt and pepper
- ¾ cup boiling red wine or water
- 1 tablespoon Dijon or other mustard
- Cayenne or red chili flakes (optional)

**Directions:**

1. Pulse the beets, dates, almonds, and ginger powder in a food processor until they are finely chopped but not nearly a paste.

2. In a large mixing basin, combine the mixture with the bulgur and a dash of salt and pepper. Place a plate over the bowl and add the cayenne, mustard, and boiling wine while stirring.

3. Let the bulgur 20 minutes to swell.

4. To taste, add salt and pepper to the dish. After forming into half-burgers and arranging on a tray without touching, refrigerate for at least an hour.

5. After turning the control knob to high, place the burgers on the griddle. Cook without rotating for ten minutes.

6. Serve with your preferred garnishes or toppers.

## Marinated Portobello Cheese Burgers

**Time to prepare:** 05 minutes
**Time to cook:** 10 minutes
**Serves:** 2
**Per Serving**: Calories 254, Fat 14 g, Sodium 496mg, Carbs 24.6g, Fiber 1.6g, Sugar 3.6g, Protein 13g

**Ingredients:**
- 4 Portobello mushroom caps
- 4 slices mozzarella cheese

- 4 buns, like brioche

**For the marinade:**
- ¼ cup balsamic vinegar
- 2 tablespoons olive oil
- 1 teaspoon dried basil
- 1 teaspoon dried oregano
- 1 teaspoon garlic powder
- ¼ teaspoon sea salt
- ¼ teaspoon black pepper

**Directions:**

1. In a large mixing basin, whisk the marinade ingredients together. Pouthe sauce over the mushroom caps to coat them.

2. After 15 minutes, rotate the container twice at room temperature.

3. Bring the griddle's temperature up to medium-high.

4. Arrange the mushrooms on the grill while reserving the marinade for basting.

5. When the meat is done, cook it for 5-8 minutes on each side.

6. Frequently brush the meat with the marinade.

7. During the last two minutes of cooking, top with mozzarella cheese.

8. Just off the griddle, serve the brioche buns.

## Garlic Parsley Cheese Sandwiches

Time to prepare: 2 minutes
Time to cook: 7 minutes
Serves: 1
**Per Serving**: Calories 555; Fat 44.7 g; Sodium 1034mg; Carbs 14.6g; Fiber 1g; Sugar 1.2g; Protein 25.8g

**Ingredients:**
- 2 slices Italian bread, sliced thin
- 2 slices provolone cheese
- 2 tablespoons butter, softened

- Garlic powder, for dusting
- Dried parsley, for dusting
- Parmesan Cheese, shredded, for dusting

**Directions:**

1. Butter two pieces of bread equally, then sprinkle garlic and parsley on each side of the seasoned bread.
2. Apply a thin layer of Parmesan cheese with a spoon on each side of the bread that has been oiled.
3. Set one piece of bread on the griddle with the greased side facing up. Heat the griddle to medium heat.
4. Add provolone slices and a second piece of bread with the butter side up.
5. Heat until bread is brown and parmesan cheese is crispy, about 3 minutes on one side and 3 minutes on the other.
6. Immediately serve with your preferred side dishes!


## Turkey Burger Patty Melts

Time to prepare: 15 minutes
Time to cook: 10 minutes
Servings: 6
**Nutritional Info:** Calories: 278; Total Fat: 9 g; Cholesterol: 63 mg; Carbohydrates: 16 g; Protein: 23 g

**Ingredients:**

- 2 pounds turkey burger patties, frozen, cooked and crumbled 1/4 cup fat-free mayonnaise
- 2 teaspoons prepared horseradish
- 6 slices (about 1/4 inch thick) or 12 slices (1/8 inch thick) sourdough bread; toasted

**Directions:**

1. Combine onion, mustard, ketchup, mayonnaise, and horseradish in a large bowl. Add crumbled hamburger patties and stir.

2. Place slices of bread on a surface. On each piece of bread, spoon 1/4 of the turkey mixture on top. Add cheese, then place the second piece of bread on top.

3. Bring a griddle to a temperature where a drop of water will bounce off of it when placed over medium heat. Sandwiches should be cooked for 3 to 5 minutes, rotating once, or until golden brown and the cheese has melted. Serve hot right away.

## Garlicky Pork Burgers

Time to prepare: 5 minutes
Time to cook: 10 minutes
Servings: 2
**Nutritional Info:** Calories 154; Fat 8g; Sodium 781mg; Carbs 18.3g; Fiber 1.6g; Sugar 3.1g; Protein 4.3g
**Ingredients:**
- ½ teaspoon salt
- ½ teaspoon black pepper
- 2 cloves garlic, chopped
- 2 hard rolls

**Directions:**
1. Pulse the meat, salt, pepper, and garlic in a food processor until it is coarsely crushed, but not much finer than chopped. (If using pre-ground beef, combine it with the salt, pepper, and garlic in a mixing bowl and stir gently with your hands.)
2. With as little handling as possible, form the beef into four 1- to 112-inch-thick patties to avoid crushing it. (This may be prepared in advance and kept chilled until you're ready to griddle it.) The burgers should be cooked on the Griddle for 10 minutes without being turned; the internal temperature should be 160°F.
3. Put food on a dish for serving.
4. Reheat the rolls in the oven.
5. Put a piece of bread in the middle of each patty.

# Cheese and Tomato Burgers

Time to prepare: 10 minutes

Time to cook: 10 minutes

Servings: 4

**Nutritional Info:** Calories 518; Fat 30.3g; Sodium 976 mg; Carbs 40.3g; Fiber 1.6g; Sugar 3.1g; Protein 22g

**Ingredients:**

- 8 slices sourdough bread
- 4 slices provolone cheese
- 4 slices yellow American cheese
- 4 slices sharp cheddar cheese
- 4 slices tomato
- 3 tablespoons mayonnaise
- 3 tablespoons butter

**Directions:**

1. Turn the griddle's heat up to medium-high.

2. Butter one side of each piece of bread and spread mayo on the other.

3. Place the cheeses on top of the griddle's greased side.

4. Lay the butter-side up the remaining bread pieces on top of the cheese.

5. Fry the second piece of bread until it is golden brown and the cheese has melted, about 10 minutes total, turning it over halfway through.

6. Slice it in half and serve it hot off the griddle.

# Vegetables and Side Dishes

## Italian Zucchini Slices

Time to prepare: 10 minutes
Time to cook: 10 minutes
Servings: 4
**Nutritional Info:** Calories: 238.78 Fat: 17.1 g Fiber: 3 g Protein: 17.5 g
**Ingredients:**

- 2 zucchini, cut into 1/2-inch thick slices 1 teaspoon Italian seasoning
- 2 garlic cloves, minced
- 1/4 cup butter, melted
- 1 1/2 tablespoons fresh parsley, chopped
- 1 tablespoon fresh lemon juice
- Pepper
- Salt

**Directions:**

1. Combine the melted butter, lemon juice, Italian seasoning, garlic, pepper, and salt in a small bowl.
2. Use the melted butter mixture to brush the zucchini slices.
3. Turn the griddle's heat to high.
4. Cook zucchini slices for 2 minutes on each side on the griddle top.
5. Place the sliced zucchini on a serving platter and top with parsley. Enjoy after serving.


## Vegetable Skewers

Time to prepare: 20 minutes
Time to cook: 14 minutes
Servings: 4
**Ingredients:**

- 1 Red Pepper, cubed

- 1 zucchini, sliced
- 1 yellow or summer squash, sliced
- 10 Bella mushrooms
- 1 Red Onion Diced
- Oil
- Seasonings

**Directions:**

1. First, soak your wooden skewers in water for around 10 minutes.
2. Next, preheat the griddle over medium-high heat for approximately 5 minutes.
3. As the griddle is heating up, season the vegetables and brush or rub the oil over them. These ought to be inserted into the skewers.
4. Using a vegetable skewer, cook on the griddle for 10 to 14 minutes.
5. Flipping is often carried out throughout the cooking stage. Add more oil and spices if necessary.
6. Plate, present, and enjoy yourself!

## Vegetable Yakisoba

Time to prepare: 10 minutes
Time to cook: 15 minutes
Servings: 8
**Nutritional Info:** Calories 266, Total fat 14g, Protein 33g, Carbs 2g
**Ingredients:**
**Sauce**

- 2 tbsp soy sauce
- 4 tbsp water
- 2 tbsp mirin
- 1 teaspoon sesame oil
- 2 teaspoon minced garlic
- 2 teaspoon chili garlic sauce
- 1 teaspoon sriracha

- 2 tbsp brown sugar
- 1/2 teaspoon ground ginger
- 1 tbsp cornstarch
- 1 teaspoon canola oil

**Stir-Fry**

- 3-4 tbsp oil
- 1/2 cup of sliced onions
- 1 sliced bell pepper
- 1 cup of chopped broccoli
- 1 cup of sliced zucchini
- 1/2 cup of matchstick carrots
- 1 handful of baby spinach (optional)
- 17 ounces of fresh yakisoba noodles

**Directions:**

1. In a mixing bowl, combine all of the sauce's components and whisk to combine. Set aside.

2. Heat your griddle to medium-high heat, add one tablespoon of oil anda few drops of sesame oil, and start stir-frying the veggies right away until they are crisp-tender (about 3-4 minutes). The griddle should bturned off, covered, and set away.

3. Add the noodles, veggies, and shrimp to the hot griddle along with the last tablespoon of oil. After swirling for a minute, pour in the sauce.

4. Continue stirring until the sauce has thickened, keeping as much of it on the noodles (and out of the oil bucket) as you can, and then serve straight immediately.

## Grilled Vegetables

Time to prepare: 15 minutes
Time to cook: 30 minutes
Servings: 4
**Nutritional Info:** Calories 266, Total fat 14g, Protein 33g, Carbs 2g

**Ingredients:**
- 2 sliced zucchini
- 2 sliced yellow squash
- 1 (cut into cubes) red pepper
- 1 Pound halved mushroom
- 1 halved and sliced onion
- 2 cups of broccoli florets
- 2 cups of cauliflower florets
- lightly sprinkle with olive oil
- 3 tbsp fresh lemon juice
- 8 garlic cloves
- 1 tbsp chopped fresh basil
- 1/4 cup of chopped parsley
- 1/2teaspoon oregano
- salt
- pepper

**Directions:**
1. Layering two huge sheets of heavy-duty tin foil Add veggies in 2.
2. Combine the ingredients for the dressing and sprinkling over the vegetables.
3. Seal the tin foil by folding it in half.
4. Grill the package with the cover on for 30 minutes over medium heat.
5. Cut the foil into serving-sized pieces.


## Fried Rice on the Griddle

Time to prepare: 10 minutes
Time to cook: 10 minutes
**Servings:** 2
**Ingredients:**
- 2 cups of white rice
- 1 every minced Carrot

- 1 chopped onion
- 1 cup of fresh peas
- 1 tbsp minced garlic
- 4 every egg
- 1 few drops of sesame oil
- 1 few drops of soy sauce
- 1 few drops of oyster sauce (optional)

**Directions:**

1. Prepare two cups of chilled white rice to start. Any kind of rice will do; we like Jasmine.

2. Sauté carrots, onions, peas, and garlic over high heat on a griddle that has been well-oiled. Get rid of the heat.

3. After whisking an egg with a few drops of toasted sesame oil, pour the mixture onto the griddle. As it starts to puff up, turn it over and cut it.

4. After adding the veggies to the cold rice, come back to the griddle.

5. Stir in a few drops of soy sauce, oyster sauce, and toasted sesame oil after the rice is heated.

6. Add the scrambled egg, then turn off the heat and plate.

## Lemon Garlic Artichokes

Time to prepare: 10 minutes
Time to cook: 15 minutes
Servings: 4
**Nutritional Info:** Calcium: 47 mg Magnesium: 39 mg Phosphorus: 344 mg Iron: 2.77 mg Potassium: 575 mg Sodium: 98 mg Zinc: 7.04 mg

**Ingredients:**

- 1/2 lemon Juice
- 1/2 cup canola oil
- 3 garlic cloves, chopped
- Sea salt

- Freshly ground black pepper
- 2 large artichokes, trimmed and halved

**Directions:**

1. Turn the griddle to the medium-high setting.

2. While the device is heating up, mix the lemon juice, oil, and garlic in a medium bowl. Before brushing the artichoke halves with the lemon-garlic mixture, season them with salt and pepper.

3. Lay the artichokes, cut side down, on the griddle. Press them down gently. Fry until blistered on both sides, 8 to 10 minutes, basting often and liberally with the lemon-garlic mixture.

## Blistered Green Beans

Time to prepare: 10 minutes

Time to cook: 10 minutes

Servings: 4

**Nutritional Info:** Calcium: 55 mg Magnesium: 47 mg Phosphorus: 363 mg Iron: 3.11 mg Potassium: 701 mg Sodium: 198 mg Zinc: 7.02 mg

**Ingredients:**

- 1 pound haricots verts or green beans, trimmed
- 2 tablespoons vegetable oil
- Juice of 1 lemon
- Pinch red pepper flakes
- Flaky sea salt
- Freshly ground black pepper

**Directions:**

1. Turn the griddle to the medium-high setting. In a medium bowl, mix the green beans with the oil until they are well coated while the appliance is preheating.

2. Put the green beans on the griddle and cook, stirring regularly, for 8 to 10 minutes, or until blistered all over. Once they have finished frying, spread them out on a big serving plate.

3. Drizzle the green beans with lemon juice, sprinkle red pepper flakes on top, and season with sea salt and black pepper.

## Steamed Carrots in Ranch Dressing

Preparetion time: 15 minutes
Time to cook: 20 minutes
Serves: 5
**Per Serving**: Calories 304, Fat 14.9g, Sodium 304mg, Carbs 12g, Fiber 6g, Sugar 2g, Protein 21g

**Ingredients:**
- 12 petite carrots
- 1 packet dry ranch dressing/seasoning mix
- 2 olive oil
- Water

**Directions:**
1. Spray cooking spray on the griddle's cooking surface.
2. Switch the four burners to medium heat and crank the knobs.
3. Let the griddle 5 minutes to heat up.
4. Combine carrots, olive oil, and ranch seasoning blend in a good bowl.
5. Stir well to ensure that all of the carrots are uniformly covered with oiand spices.
6. Add the carrots to the griddle and cook for about 3 minutes, stirring now and again.
7. To create steam, add 3 tablespoons of water to the pile of carrots.
8. Use a metal dish or basting cover to cover the mound of carrots.
9. To continue steaming the carrots, toss them, add a few tablespoons
of water, and re-cover with basting marinade.
10. Boil carrots for 12 minutes or until desired softness is achieved.
11. Serve.

# Zucchini Squash Mix

Time to prepare: 15 minutes
Time to cook: 10 minutes
Serves: 6
**Per Serving**: Calories 381, Fat 21g, Sodium 561mg, Carbs 21g, Fiber 6.1g, Sugar 5g, Protein 32g
**Ingredients:**

- 2 zucchini, diced
- 2 squash, diced
- 1 large onion, diced
- 2-3 tomatoes on the vine, diced
- 5-6 garlic cloves, roughly chopped
- 1 can cannelloni beans, drained
- Olive oil
- Black pepper and salt to taste

**Istructions:**

1. In a good dish, toss all the vegetables and beans with salt and blackpepper.

2. Spray cooking spray on the griddle's cooking surface.

3. Switch the four burners to medium heat and turn on the burners.

4. Let the Griddle to warm up for five minutes.

5. Place the vegetable combination on the griddle top and cook it until it is tender.

6. Serve.


# Sautéed Savoury Green Beans

Time to prepare: 15 minutes
Time to cook: 20 minutes
Serves: 6

**Per Serving**: Calories 339, Fat 13g; Sodium 421mg, Carbs 16g, Fiber 4.1g, Sugar 3.2g, Protein 27g

**Ingredients:**
- 2 lbs. fresh green beans
- 1 tablespoon of olive oil
- 1 teaspoon of garlic powder
- Black pepper and salt to taste

**Istructions:**
1. Combine all the ingredients for the recipe in a dish and stir until the beans are well covered.
2. Spray cooking spray on the griddle's cooking surface.
3. Switch the four burners to medium-high heat and turn on the burners.
4. Let the Griddle to warm up for five minutes.
5. Spread the beans out on the griddle and cook for 20 minutes, stirring occasionally.
6. Serve.
7. On a griddle, cook beans until they are the required softness, stirring occasionally.

## Easy Seared Green Beans

Time to prepare: 10 minutes
Time to cook: 10 minutes
Servings: 6
**Nutritional Info:**  Calories 266, Total fat 14g, Protein 33g, Carbs 2g
**Ingredients:**
- 1 1/2 lbs green beans, trimmed
- 1 1/2 tablespoons rice vinegar
- 3 tablespoons soy sauce
- 1 1/2 tablespoons sesame oil
- 2 tablespoons sesame seeds, toasted
- 1 1/2 tablespoons brown sugar

- 1/4 teaspoons black pepper

**Directions:**

1. After 3 minutes of cooking, drain the beans carefully.
2. Drain the green beans once more after placing them in cold ice water. Towel-dry the green beans.
3. Turn the griddle's heat to high.
4. Saturate the heated griddle surface with oil.
5. Stir-fry the green beans for 2 minutes.
6. Stir fry for a further 2 minutes before adding the soy sauce, brown sugar, vinegar, and pepper.
7. Stir the sesame seeds well to coat. Enjoy after serving.

## Grilled Hash Browns

Time to prepare: 10 minutes
Time to cook: 30 minutes
Servings: 4

**Ingredients:**

- 4 Tbsp unsalted softened butter
- 20 Ounces shredded hash brown potatoes thawed if frozen 1 large seeded and diced green bell pepper ½ cup of diced white or yellow onion
- 2 cloves garlic minced or chopped
- ½ teaspoon kosher salt
- ¼ teaspoon fresh cracked pepper
- 4 large eggs
- garnish: chopped flat-leaf parsley

**Directions:**

1. Prepare the griddle by cleaning and seasoning it before usage.
2. After everything is prepared, turn the heat down to medium.
3. Combine all the ingredients on a tray before adding them on the griddle. Combine the potatoes, green bell pepper, onion, and garlic in a mixing bowl.

4. Melt the butter on the griddle. The griddle has to be hot enough so that the butter quickly melts and sizzles without burning.

5. Combine the potatoes, green bell pepper, onion, and garlic in a large bowl and toss to combine. Cook, often rotating the potatoes, until they are just just (but not quite) done (about 5 minutes). Be careful not toss the potatoes too much since they must quickly brown on the hot griddle. Every so often, taste the food to see whether it is done.

6. After sprinkling with salt and pepper, stack the potatoes on a mound that is 12 to 7 inches wide. Use a fork or spoon to poke four wells into the potatoes. Gently crack an egg into each well. Cook with a frying dome while covered.

8. Immediately serve with a garnish of parsley.

## Crispy Cooked Potatoes

Time to prepare: 15 minutes
Time to cook: 25 minutes
Servings: 6
**Nutritional Info:** Calories 416; Fat 11g; Sodium 501mg; Carbs 16g; Fiber 2.1g; Sugar 2.2g; Protein 28g
**Ingredients:**

- 6 potatoes, diced
- 2 tablespoons olive oil
- 2 teaspoons of black pepper
- 2 ½ teaspoons of garlic powder
- 2 teaspoons of dried rosemary
- Salt to taste

**Directions:**

1Sliced potatoes should be boiled in a sufficient saucepan until fork-tender.

2. Drain the potatoes and place them in an appropriate basin. Add salt, rosemary, black pepper, garlic powder, and olive oil. Toss potatoes until they are completely covered.

3. Spray cooking spray on the griddle's cooking surface.

4. Switch the four burners to medium heat and turn on the burners.

5. Let the griddle 5 minutes to warm up.

6. Place the potatoes on the griddle and cook for 5 to 6 minutes on each side, or until crispy.

7. Serve.

## Parmesan Zucchini

Time to prepare: 15 minutes
Time to cook: 15 minutes
Servings: 4
**Nutritional Info:** Calories 338; Fat 12g; Sodium 521mg; Carbs 14g; Fiber 5.1g; Sugar 3g; Protein 27g

**Ingredients:**
- 3 medium zucchinis, sliced
- 1 tablespoon of olive oil
- 1 tablespoon of grated parmesan cheese
- ½ teaspoon of garlic powder
- ¼ teaspoon of black pepper

**Directions:**
1. Spray cooking spray on the griddle's cooking surface.

2. Switch the four burners to medium heat and crank the knobs.

3. Let the griddle 5 minutes to heat up.

4. Add the zucchini slices, and simmer for approximately 3 minutes, stirring occasionally.

5. After the zucchini is soft, stir in the parmesan cheese, garlic powder, and pepper.

6. Serve.

## Fried Green Tomatoes with Parsley

Time to prepare: 10 minutes
Time to cook: 10 minutes

Servings: 1

**Nutritional Info:** Calories 304; Fat 14.9g; Sodium 304mg; Carbs 12g; Fiber 6g; Sugar 2g; Protein 21g

**Ingredients:**

- 4 green tomatoes
- 3 cups of Italian style bread crumbs
- 2 cups of flour
- 2 teaspoons of garlic powder
- 3 eggs
- ½ cup of milk
- Black pepper and salt to taste
- Parsley garnish, chopped
- Lemon zest garnish
- 3 tablespoons of butter
- 2 ½ tablespoons of flour

**Directions:**

1. In a good bowl, whisk three eggs with a half cup of milk, salt, and black pepper.
2. Combine 2 cups of flour and 2 teaspoons of garlic powder.
3. On a dish, scatter breadcrumbs with Italian seasoning.
4. Cut tomatoes into 1/4 to 12 inch-thick slices.
5. Evenly coat the slices in the flour mixture, brushing off any extra.
6. After that, dip the slices into the egg wash, coat them uniformly, and then press them into the breadcrumbs.
7. Spray cooking spray on the griddle's cooking surface.
8. Switch the four burners to medium heat and turn on the burners.
9. Let the griddle 5 minutes to heat up.

The coated tomato slices should be placed on the griddle top and cooked for 5 to 11 minutes on each side.

12. Serve.

**Tasty Cornish Game Hen**

Time to prepare: 10 minutes
Time to cook: 10 minutes
Servings: 4
**Nutritional Info:** Calories 378; Fat 15g; Sodium 521mg; Carbs 14g; Fiber 5.1g; Sugar 3g; Protein 27g
**Ingredients:**

- 1 Cornish game hen
- ½ tablespoons of olive oil
- ¼ tablespoon of poultry seasoning

**Directions:**

1. Spray cooking spray on the griddle's cooking surface.
2. Switch the four burners to medium-high heat and crank the knobs.
3. Let the griddle 5 minutes to heat up.

4. Oil the hen and season it with poultry seasoning.
5. Put the hen on the top of the hot griddle, and cook it until it is browned on both sides.
6. Smoke the bird for 60 minutes, or until the internal temperature reaches 180°F, while covering it with a lid or pan.
7. Serve.

# Poultry Recipes

## California Seared Chicken

Time to prepare: 35 minutes
Time to cook: 20 minutes
Servings: 4
**Nutritional Info:** Calories: 230 Protein: 37.5 g Carbs: 2.2 g Fat: 7 g
Sugar: 1.3 g
**Ingredients:**

- 4 boneless, skinless chicken breasts
- 3/4 cup balsamic vinegar
- 2 tablespoons extra virgin olive oil
- 1 tablespoon honey
- 1 teaspoon oregano
- 1 teaspoon basil
- 1 teaspoon garlic powder
- For garnish:
- Sea salt to taste
- Black pepper, fresh ground to taste
- 4 slices fresh mozzarella cheese
- 4 slices avocado
- 4 slices beefsteak tomato
- Balsamic glaze, for drizzling

**Directions:**

1. Combine the balsamic vinegar, honey, olive oil, oregano, basil, and garlic powder in a large mixing basin.
2. After coating, add the chicken, and marinate it for 30 minutes in the refrigerator.
3. Set the heat on the griddle to medium-high. Till a meat thermometer reads 165°F, 7 minutes on each side.
Chicken should be seared using 4.

5. Mozzarella, avocado, and tomato should be sprinkled on top of each chicken breast. For two minutes, wrap foil around the griddle to let the cheese melt.

6. As a last touch, add some balsamic glaze and season with sea salt and black pepper.

## Chili Lime Chicken with Sesame Seed

Preparetion time: 35 minutes

Time to cook: 15 minutes

Serves: 4

**Nutritional Info:** Calories 950| Fat 33.7 g| Sodium 1541 mg| Carbs 18.4g| Fiber 0.2g| Sugar 16g| Protein 132.2g

**Ingredients:**

- ½ cup sweet chili sauce
- ¼ cup soy sauce
- 1-teaspoon mirin
- ½-teaspoon orange juice
- 1-teaspoon orange marmelade
- 1-tablespoon lime juice
- 1 tbsp. brown sugar
- 1 clove garlic, minced
- 4-pound Boneless chicken breasts
- Sesame seeds, for garnish

**Istructions:**

1. Combine the soy sauce, brown sugar, sweet chili sauce, orange marmalade, mirin, lime and orange juice, and chopped garlic in a good mixing dish.

2. Save aside 1/4 cup of this sauce.

3. Combine the remaining sauce with the chicken, coat thoroughly, and set aside for 30 minutes.

4. minute marinating period.

5. Set the griddle's knob to the medium-heat position to preheat it.

6. Spray cooking spray on the griddle's top.

7. Put the chicken on the heated griddle surface and cook it for 7 minutes on each side.

8. Add sesame seeds as a garnish and serve.

## Seared Spicy Boneless Chicken Thighs

Preparetion time: **8-24 hours**
Time to cook: 20 minutes
Serves: 4
**Nutritional Info:** Calories 559| Fat 23.8 g| Sodium 430 mg| Carbs 18.3g| Fiber 0.3g| Sugar 17.6g| Protein 65.8g
**Ingredients:**
- 2-pound boneless chicken thighs
- ¼ cup fresh lime juice
- 2-teaspoon lime zest
- ¼ cup honey
- 2 tablespoons olive oil
- ½-tablespoon balsamic vinegar
- ½-teaspoon sea salt
- ½-teaspoon black pepper
- ½ Garlic cloves, minced
- ¼-teaspoon onion powder

**Istructions:**
1. Combine all the marinade ingredients in a good mixing basin; save 2 tablespoons for basting.
2. Place the chicken and marinate in a plastic bag that can be sealed, shake, and store in the fridge overnight.
3. Set the griddle's knob to the medium-heat position to preheat it.

4. Apply frying oil to the griddle top.

5. On the heated griddle top, cook the marinated chicken for 8 minutes on each side while basting.

6. Dish out and savor!

## Honey Balsamic Marinated Chicken

Time to prepare: 30 minutes – 4 hours
Time to cook: 20 minutes
Servings: 4
**Nutritional Info:** Calories: 485 Sodium: 438 mg Dietary Fiber: 0.5 g Fat: 18.1 g Carbs: 11 g Protein: 66.1 g

**Ingredients:**
- 2 lbs. boneless, skinless chicken thighs
- 1 teaspoon olive oil
- 1/2 teaspoon sea salt
- 1/4 teaspoon black pepper
- 1/2 teaspoon paprika
- 3/4 teaspoon onion powder
- For the Marinade:
- 2 tablespoons honey
- 2 tablespoons balsamic vinegar
- 2 tablespoons tomato paste
- 1 teaspoon garlic, minced

**Directions:**

1. Fill a plastic bag with the following ingredients: chicken, olive oil, salt, black pepper, paprika, and onion powder. Set aside after sealing and coating the chicken with seasonings and oil.

2. Combine tomato paste, honey, garlic, and balsamic vinegar in a bowl.

3. Equally split the marinade in two. The remaining half should be kept in a refrigerator-safe container after adding the first half to the bag of chicken.

4. Close the bag, then shake the chicken to coat. For a period of 30 to 45 minutes, refrigerate.
Set a griddle to medium-high heat.
7. Discard the marinade and bag. Cook the chicken on the griddle for 7 to 8 minutes on each side, or until a meat thermometer registers 165°F.
9. Serve right away.

## Herb Roasted Turkey in Chicken Broth

Time to prepare: 15 minutes
Time to cook: 3 hrs. 35 minutes
Serves: 12
**Per Serving**: Calories 376; Fat 13g; Sodium 421mg; Carbs 16g; Fiber 4.1g; Sugar 3.2g; Protein 27g
**Ingredients:**
- Fourteen pounds of turkey, cleaned
- 2 tablespoons of chopped mixed herbs
- ¼ teaspoon of ground black pepper, to taste
- 3 tablespoons of butter, unsalted, melted
- 2 cups of chicken broth

**Istructions:**
1. Spray cooking spray on the griddle's cooking surface.
2. Switch the four burners to medium heat and crank the knobs.
3. Let the griddle 5 minutes to heat up.
4. Before putting the turkey on a roasting pan and tucking the wings with butcher's thread, remove the giblets, wash the bird inside and out, and then pat it dry with paper towels.
5. In the meanwhile, prepare herb butter by combining melted butter with black pepper and chopped herbs in a suitable basin and whisking until foamy.
6. Spread some of the prepared herb butter under the turkey's skin using the handle of a wooden spoon, then massage the skin to distribute the butter evenly.

7. After seasoning the turkey with the pork and poultry rub and massaging melted butter all over its exterior, place it in a roasting pan.

Remove the cover once the griddle is heated, place the roasting pan with the turkey on the grate, cover the griddle, and smoke for 3 hours and 30 minutes, or until the internal temperature of the meat reaches 165 degrees F and the top is golden brown.

Once the turkey has finished cooking, transfer it to a cutting board and allow it to rest there for 30 minutes before slicing it and serving.

12. Serve.

## Butterflied Chicken

Time to prepare: 15 minutes
Time to cook: 50 minutes
Servings: 6
**Nutritional Info:** Calories 507, Total Fat 17.1 g, Saturated Fat 4 g, Cholesterol 227 mg, Sodium 162 mg, Total Carbs 0.8 g, Fiber 0.1 g, Sugar 0.1 g, Protein 82.2 g

**Ingredients:**

- 1 (3½-4-pound) whole chicken, neck and giblets removed 3 tablespoons fresh lime juice
- 2 tablespoons extra-virgin olive oil
- 1 tablespoon garlic, minced
- 2 teaspoons lime zest, freshly grated 3 tablespoons Mexican chili powder
- 1 teaspoon ground coriander
- 1 teaspoon ground cuminutes
- Salt and ground black pepper, as required

**Directions:**

1. Place the chicken breast-side down on a large chopping board.
2. To flip the chicken, start at the thigh and use kitchen shears to cut down one side of the backbone.
3. Next, remove the backbone by cutting along the other side.
4. Alternate the side, open it like a book, and then forcefully flatten the backbone.
5. Combine the lime juice, oil, garlic, lime zest, chili powder, coriander, cumin, salt, and black pepper in a clean glass bowl.
6. Distribute the spice mixture evenly over the chicken.
7. Place plastic wrap over the chicken and refrigerate for about 24 hours.
9. Heat the Outdoor Gas Griddle to medium-high heat on half of it while leaving the other half unheated.
10. Put the skin-side-down marinated chicken on the hot griddle and cook for approximately 5 minutes.
11. After cooking for approximately 5 minutes, flip the chicken.
12. Next, put the chicken on the griddle's side that hasn't been cooked and cover it with the cooking dome.
13. Cook for about 30 to 40 minutes, or until well cooked.
14. Take the chicken from the griddle and let it aside for 10 minutes before cutting.
15. Divide the chicken into serving-size pieces.


## Lemony Chicken Breast

Time to prepare: 15 minutes
Time to cook: 16 minutes
Servings: 6
**Nutritional Info:** Calories 434, Total Fat 28.1 g, Saturated Fat 5.6 g, Cholesterol 135 mg, Sodium 159 mg, Total Carbs 0.4 g, Fiber 0.1 g, Sugar 0.2 g, Protein 43.9 g
**Ingredients:**
- ½ cup olive oil
- ¼ cup fresh lemon juice

- 1 garlic clove, minced
- Salt and ground black pepper, as required
- 2 pounds boneless, skinless chicken breasts

**Directions:**

1. To make the marinade, mix the oil, lemon juice, garlic, salt, and black pepper in a large basin.
2. Put the chicken breasts and marinate in a large plastic bag that can be sealed.
3. Close the bag and shake to thoroughly coat.
4. Keep chilled the next day.
5. Turn the outside gas griddle's heat to medium.
6. Liberally grease the griddle.
7. Take the chicken breasts out of the bag and throw the marinade away.
8. Put a cooking dome over the griddle and add the chicken breasts.
9. Cook for around 6 to 8 minutes on each side.
10. Present hot.

## Marinated Chicken Breast

Time to prepare: 1 hr 0 minutes
Time to cook: 15 min
Servings: 1

**Ingredients:**

- 12 Ounces (Boneless, Skinless) Chicken Breast Italian Dressing 5 Ounces

**Directions:**

1. Combine the Italian dressing and the chicken breast in a Ziplock bag.
2. Carefully poke holes in the bird.
3. Place in the fridge for up to 24 hours or at least 1–2 hours. To spread the Italian dressing evenly, rotate the chicken occasionally.
4. Chicken breast that has been marinated, and medium-low heat on the griddle.

5. Once the griddle has heated up, put the chicken breast on it. Any marinade that is left over must be thrown away.

6. Sauté the chicken for 5 minutes, or until golden brown.

7. Flip the Italian chicken breasts over and continue to cook.

8. Check the temperature of the chicken when it is nearly done using a digital thermometer. The chicken should be cooked until the thickest section reaches 165 degrees. The chicken will dry out and become tough if it is cooked over 165°.

9. When the chicken is thoroughly cooked, remove it from the griddle.

## Chicken Wings with Sweet Red Chili and Peach Glaze

Time to prepare: 15 minutes
Time to cook: 30 minutes
Servings: 4
**Nutritional Info:** Calories: 195 Fat: 7 g Saturated Fat: 1 g
Cholesterol: 60 mg Sodium: 182 mg
Carbs: 0 g Fiber: 0 g Sugar 0 g Protein: 31.6 g
**Ingredients:**
- 1 (12 oz.) jar peach preserves
- 1 cup sweet red chili sauce
- 1 teaspoon lime juice
- 1 tablespoon fresh cilantro, minced
- 1 (2-1/2 lb.) bag chicken wing sections
- Non-stick cooking spray

**Directions:**
1. In a mixing bowl, combine preserves, red chili sauce, lime juice, and cilantro.
2. Split in half, setting aside one half for serving.
3. Spray a medium-hot griddle with nonstick cooking spray before heating it up.
4. After 25 minutes, flip the wings several times to ensure that the juices flow clean.

5. Take the wings from the griddle and toss them in a dish with the remaining glaze to coat them.

6. Add the wings back to the griddle and cook for 3 to 5 more minutes, rotating once.

Warm up and serve with your preferred sides and dips!

## Blackstone Chicken Phillies

Time to prepare: 10 min
Time to cook: 15 min
Servings: 6

**Ingredients:**

- 2 Tbsps vegetable oil
- 2 pounds of chicken breasts (thin strips)
- 2 onions thinly sliced
- 8 Ounces sliced mushrooms
- kosher salt, pepper, Old Bay seasoning
- 1 to 2 Tbsps worcestershire sauce
- 1/2 cup of sliced banana peppers
- 3 cloves garlic minced
- 6 hoagy/ sub buns
- 12 slices provolone cheese
- 1/2 cup of mayo

**Directions:**

1. Set the Blackstone grill to medium-high for a few minutes to pre-heat.

2. Apply a tablespoon of vegetable oil to the grill's two long sides. Put the onions and mushrooms on one side of the pan, then the chicken on the other.

3. Season the chicken, onions, and mushrooms with kosher salt, blackpepper, and Old Bay seasoning. Worcestershire sauce is then

used to season both the chicken and the onions/mushrooms after cooking for 6to 8 minutes while rotating and flipping the pan a few times.

4. Combine the chicken, onions, and mushrooms on the flat top grill.

5. In a mixing dish, combine the garlic and banana peppers. Cook for a further 6 to 8 minutes while once or twice twisting and rotating the pan.

7. Toast the buns on the grill for a minute or two, cut side down.

8. Add 2 slices of provolone to the top of 6 piles of chicken and veggie on the grill, then turn it off.

9. Once the cheese has melted, spread mayo on a bun.

## Teriyaki Chicken Stir Fry

Time to prepare: 5 min
Time to cook: 10 min
Total time: 15 min

**Ingredients:**
- Chicken Breast
- Favorite Veggies (fresh is obviously best, but stir fry blended veggies can be bought frozen)
- Teriyaki Sauce
- Extra Virgin Olive Oil
- White Rice (Optional, but a great addition)

**Directions:**
The chicken breast should first be cut into tiny pieces and placed in a basin.

2. Put each of your finely chopped veggies in its own bowl.

3. Make your own teriyaki sauce from scratch or buy a pre-made bottle from the shop.

4. Place the chicken on the griddle, oil one side, and heat to high.

5. Cook the chicken for 2 minutes, turning it over halfway through. Spread the vegetables and a little oil on the griddle's other side.
6. Grill the chicken and vegetables separately until the chicken registers a temperature of 165 degrees inside (turning regularly).
7. After the chicken has reached the required minimum internal temperature, combine it with the veggies on the Blackstone.
8. Stirring often, add half of the teriyaki sauce first, then the other half. At this point, the Teriyaki Chicken Stir Fry is complete. Take the chicken out and either eat it simply or serve it over a bed of white rice.

## Blackstone Chicken Teriyaki

Time to prepare: 10 minutes
Time to cook: 10 minutes
Servings: 4
**Ingredients:**
- 1 1/2 pounds chicken thighs or chicken breasts (boneless & skinless ) 4 cloves garlic minced
- 1/2 cup of teriyaki sauce
- 1 red bell pepper
- 1 yellow bell pepper
- 1 onion
- 8 oz mushrooms
- vegetable oil for the griddle
- kosher salt, pepper
- Optional: sesame seeds, green onions, more teriyaki sauce

**Directions:**
1. In a gallon plastic bag, combine the chicken pieces, minced garlic, and 1/4 cup of teriyaki sauce. To evenly spread the contents, massage the bag. Overnight or in the refrigerator.
2. Slice the bell peppers, onion, and mushrooms very thinly.

3. Turn on your griddle and adjust the heat to medium-high. Add the chicken, veggies, and the last 1/4 cup of teriyaki sauce to the heated pan. When required, add kosher salt and pepper.

4. Cook, sometimes tossing, for 7 to 9 minutes.

5. If desired, add more teriyaki sauce, sesame seeds, and green onions to the top.


## Sizzling Chicken Fajitas

Time to prepare: 5 minutes
Time to cook: 25 minutes
Servings: 4
**Nutritional Info:** Calories: 398 Protein: 52 g Carbs: 20 g Fat: 18 g
**Ingredients:**
- 4 boneless chicken breast halves, thinly sliced
- 1 yellow onion, sliced
- 1 large green bell pepper, sliced
- 1 large red bell pepper, sliced
- 1 teaspoon ground cuminutes
- 1 teaspoon garlic powder
- 1 teaspoon onion powder
- 2 tablespoons lime juice
- 1 tablespoon olive oil
- 1/2 teaspoon black pepper
- 1 teaspoon salt
- 2 tablespoons vegetable oil
- 10 flour tortillas

**Directions:**
1. Combine the chicken, cumin, garlic, onion, lime juice, salt, pepper, and olive oil in a zip-top bag. 30 minutes is enough time to marinate.
2. Heat the griddle to medium.
3. Place the olive oil on the griddle's one side and heat until shimmering.

4. Add the pepper and onion and sauté until they start to soften.

5. Place the marinated chicken on the opposite side of the griddle and cook until just browned.

6. Once the chicken has been gently browned, combine it with the onion and pepper and simmer until the internal temperature of the chicken reaches 165°F.

7. Take the chicken and veggies off the griddle, and then serve them on tortillas that are still warm.

## Hawaiian Chicken Skewers

Time to prepare: 70 minutes

Time to cook: 15 minutes

Servings: 4

**Nutritional Info:** Calories: 230 Protein: 28 g Carbs: 2 g Fat: 14 g

**Ingredients:**

- 3 lb. chicken breast, cut into 1 ½ inch cubes 2 cups pineapple, cut into 1 ½ inch cubes
- 2 large green peppers, cut into 1 ½ inch pieces
- 1 large red onion, cut into 1 ½ inch pieces
- 2 tablespoons olive oil, to coat veggies For the marinade:
- 1/3 cup tomato paste
- 1/3 cup brown sugar, packed
- 1/3 cup soy sauce
- 1/4 cup pineapple juice
- 2 tablespoons olive oil
- 1 1/2 tablespoon mirin or rice wine vinegar
- 2 teaspoons garlic cloves, minced
- 1 tablespoon ginger, minced
- 1/2 teaspoon sesame oil
- Pinch of sea salt
- Pinch of ground black pepper
- 10 wooden skewers, for assembly

**Directions:**

1. Blend the marinade ingredients in a mixing basin. Half of the marinade should be kept in the fridge.
2. Place the chicken and leftover marinade in a plastic bag that can be sealed, and chill for an hour.
3. Turn the griddle's heat to medium.
4. Add 2 5 teaspoons of olive oil to a mixing bowl along with the red onion, bell pepper, and pineapple and toss to coat.
6. When all of the chicken is gone, thread pineapple, bell pepper, red onion, and chicken onto the skewers.
7. Arrange the skewers on the griddle and get the marinade you set aside from the fridge. Cook for 5 minutes, then brush with the leftover marinade and turn.
8. Reapply the marinade and continue to sear the chicken for approximately 5 more minutes, or until the internal temperature of the chicken reaches 165°F.
9. Serve hot.

## Fiery Italian Chicken Skewers

Time to prepare: 80 minutes
Time to cook: 20 minutes
Servings: 4
**Nutritional Info:** Calories: 945 Sodium: 798 mg Dietary Fiber: 3.2 g
Fat: 46.7 g Carbs: 14.7 g Protein: 112.2 g
**Ingredients:**

- 10 chicken thighs, 1 red onion, cut into wedges
- 1 red pepperFor the marinade:
- 1/3 cup pine nuts
- 1 1/2 cups red peppers
- 2 Hot cherry peppers, stemmed and seeded, or to taste 1 cup packed fresh basil leaves, plus more to serve cloves garlic, peeled 1/4 cup grated Parmesan cheese
- 1 tablespoon paprika
- Extra virgin olive oil, as needed

**Directions:**

1. Combine the toasted pine nuts, roasted red peppers, hot cherry peppers, basil, garlic, Parmesan, and paprika in a food processor or blender. Blend until completely smooth.

2. Add olive oil to the pesto until it gets thin before using it as a marinade for the chicken.

3. Transfer the remaining pesto to a large sealable plastic bag and set aside half of it for serving.

4. Put the chopped chicken thighs to the pesto bag, lock it, and shake to cover the meat.

5. Let food chill for an hour.

6. Brush olive oil on the griddle and heat it to medium-high.

7. Red onion, red pepper, and chicken pieces are threaded onto metal skewers.

8. Spread the chicken with the leftover pesto.

9. Sauté the chicken for approximately 5 minutes on each side, or until the internal temperature reaches 165°F. Serve warm with your favorite salad or vegetables!

# Turkey Recipes

## Cured Turkey Drumstick

Time to prepare: 10 minutes
Time to cook: 45 minutes
Servings: 3
**Nutritional Info:** Calories 266, Total fat 14g, Protein 33g, Carbs 2g
**Ingredients:**
- 3 fresh or thawed frozen turkey drumsticks
- 3 tablespoons of olive oil

For the brine
- 4 cups of filtered water
- ¼ cup of kosher salt, to taste
- ¼ cup of brown sugar
- 1 teaspoon of garlic powder
- 1 teaspoon of poultry seasoning
- ½ teaspoon of red pepper flakes
- 1 teaspoon of pink hardened salt

**Directions:**
1. Fill a 1-gallon bag that can be sealed with the salt water components.
2. Place the salted water with the turkey drumstick in the refrigerator for 12 hours.
3. Take the drumstick out of the saline after 12 hours, give it a cold water rinse, and then wipe it dry with a paper towel.
4. Let the drumstick to air dry for two hours in the refrigerator without a cover.
5. Take the drumsticks out of the fridge and coat each one with a tablespoon of olive oil.
6. Spray cooking spray on the griddle's cooking surface.
7. Switch the four burners to medium heat and turn on the burners.
8. Let the griddle 5 minutes to heat up.

9. Arrange the drumstick on the griddle and cook it for 20 minutes on each side.

10. Using an instant reading digital thermometer, cook the turkey drumsticks at 325°F until the thickest section of each drumstick reaches 180°F internally.

11. For 15 minutes before to consumption, place a smoked turkey drumstick in a loose foil tent.

12. Serve.

## Bourbon Turkey

Time to prepare: 15 minutes
Time to cook: 3 hours
Servings: 8)
**Nutritional Info:** Calories 266, Total fat 14g, Protein 33g, Carbs 2g
**Ingredients:**

- 8 cups of chicken broth
- 1 stick of butter softened
- 1 teaspoon of thyme
- 1 (12 pounds) turkey
- 2 garlic cloves, minced
- 1 teaspoon of dried basil
- 1 teaspoon of pepper
- 1 teaspoon of salt
- 1 tablespoon of minced rosemary
- 1 teaspoon of paprika
- 1 lemon (wedged)
- 1 onion
- 1 apple (wedged)
- 1 orange (wedged)
- Maple bourbon glaze
- ¾ cup of bourbon
- ½ cup of maple syrup

- 1 stick of butter (melted)
- 1 tablespoon of lime

**Directions:**

1. Wash the turkey flesh from inside out under cold running water.
2. Insert the lemon, onion, apple, and orange into the turkey's cavity.
3. In a good mixing bowl, combine the paprika, butter, thyme, basil, garlic, pepper, salt, and rosemary
4. Place a rack and the turkey on the rack in a roasting pan.
6. Spray cooking spray on the griddle's cooking surface.
7. Switch the four burners to medium heat and turn on the burners.
8. Let the griddle 5 minutes to heat up.
9. Using the covered roasting pan, cook on the griddle for an hour.
10. Combine all of the components for the maple bourbon glaze in a good mixing bowl. Combine all ingredients well.
11. Brush the bird with the glaze mixture. Cook and smoke the turkey for a another two hours, basting it every half-hour and adding more broth as necessary, or until the internal temperature reaches 165°F.
12. Serve.

## Brine-Marinated Turkey Breast

Time to prepare: 15 minutes
Time to cook: 90 minutes
Servings: 6
**Nutritional Info:** Calories 266, Total fat 14g, Protein 33g, Carbs 2g
**Ingredients:**

For the brine

- 1 cup of kosher salt, to taste
- 1 cup of maple syrup
- ¼ cup of brown sugar
- ¼ cup of whole black peppercorns
- 4 cups of cold bourbon

- 1 ½ gallons of cold water
- 1 turkey breast of about 7 pounds

For turkey

- 3 tablespoons of brown sugar
- 1 ½ tablespoons of smoked paprika
- 1 ½ teaspoons of chipotle chili powder
- 1 ½ teaspoons of garlic powder
- 1 ½ teaspoons of salt, to taste
- 1 ½ teaspoons of black pepper, to taste
- 1 teaspoon of onion powder
- ½ teaspoon of ground cuminutes
- 6 tablespoons of melted unsalted butter

**Directions:**

1. Ensure that the bourbon, water, and chicken stock are all cool before starting.
2. To prepare the brine, mix all of the ingredients in a big bucket: salt, syrup, sugar, peppercorns, bourbon, and water.
3. Take off any remaining parts of the turkey, such as the neck and the giblets.
4. In a sealable bag, refrigerate the turkey flesh in the brine for approximately 8 to 12 hours.
5. After removing the turkey breast, spread it out on a baking sheet, and chill it for approximately an hour.
6. Spray cooking spray on the griddle's cooking surface.
7. Switch the four burners to medium-low heat and switch on the burners.
8. Let the griddle 5 minutes to heat up.
9. Combine the paprika, sugar, chili powder, garlic powder, salt, pepper, onion powder, cumin, and an appropriate bowl with all of the other ingredients.
11. Gently remove the turkey's skin, then brush the flesh with the melted butter. The meat and skin should both be well covered with the spice.

12. Grill the turkey breast for approximately 1 1/2 hours at 375 degrees Fahrenheit.
13. Cut and present.
14. Serve.


## Smoked Turkey Tabasco

Time to prepare: 15 minutes
Time to cook: 4 hours 45 minutes
Servings: 8)
**Nutritional Info:** Calories 416; Fat 31g; Sodium 501mg; Carbs 16g; Fiber 2.1g; Sugar 2.2g; Protein 28g
**Ingredients:**
**Ingredients:**

* 1 Whole turkey (4-lbs.)

For the rub

* ¼ cup of brown sugar
* 2 teaspoons of smoked paprika
* 1 teaspoon of salt
* 1 ½ teaspoons of onion powder
* 2 teaspoons of oregano
* 2 teaspoons of garlic powder
* ½ teaspoon of dried thyme
* ½ teaspoon of white pepper
* ½ teaspoon of cayenne pepper, to taste

For the glaze

* ½ cup of ketchup
* ½ cup of hot sauce
* 1 tablespoon of cider vinegar
* 2 teaspoons of tabasco
* ½ teaspoon of Cajun spices
* 3 tablespoons of unsalted butter

**Directions:**

1. Sprinkle 2 teaspoons each of brown sugar, smoked paprika, salt, onion powder, garlic powder, dried thyme, white pepper, and cayenne pepper over the turkey before cooking. Give the turkey one hour to rest.
2. Spray cooking spray on the griddle's cooking surface.
3. Switch the four burners to low heat and turn on the burners.
4. Let the Griddle to warm up for five minutes.
5. Cook the seasoned turkey for 4 hours on the griddle.
6. In a saucepan, combine ketchup, hot sauce, cider vinegar, tabasco, and Cajun seasonings. After simmering, remove from heat.
7. Turn off the heat and rapidly stir in unsalted butter to the sauce.
8. Stir to dissolve.
9. Continue smoking the turkey for 15 minutes after 4 hours by brushing it with tabasco sauce.
10. Serve.


## Jalapeno Turkey in Broth

Time to prepare: 15 minutes
Time to cook: 3 hours 45 minutes
Servings: 4
**Nutritional Info:** Calories 318; Fat 15g; Sodium 521mg; Carbs 14g; Fiber 5.1g; Sugar 3g; Protein 27g
**Ingredients:**
- 5 pounds of the whole turkey, giblet removed
- ½ of the medium red onion, peeled and minced
- 8 jalapeño peppers
- 2 tablespoons of minced garlic
- 4 tablespoons of garlic powder
- 6 tablespoons of Italian seasoning
- 1 cup of butter, softened, unsalted
- ¼ cup of olive oil
- 1 cup of chicken broth

## Directions:

1. Heat oil and butter in a decent saucepan over medium heat. After the butter has melted, add the onion, peppers, and garlic. Cook for 3 to 5 minutes, or until the mixture is pleasantly golden brown.

3. Add the broth and stir well. After 5 minutes of boiling, turn off the heat and sift the mixture to get just the liquid.

4. Spray the exterior of the turkey with butter spray, then liberally sprinkle it with garlic salt and Italian seasoning. Inject the bird liberally with the prepared liquid.

5. Spray cooking spray on the griddle's cooking surface.

6. Switch the four burners to low heat and turn on the burners.

7. Let the griddle 5 minutes to heat up.

8. Put the turkey on the griddle, cover it with the lid, and smoke it for 30 minutes. Then, lower the heat to medium-low, and smoke it for an additional 3 hours.

9. Serve.

## Mayo Turkey

Time to prepare: 15 minutes
Time to cook: 4 hours 5 minutes
Servings: 10
**Nutritional Info:** Calories 401; Fat 13g; Sodium 161mg; Carbs 10g; Fiber 3.1g; Sugar 2g; Protein 25g

**Ingredients:**

- 1 Whole turkey (4-lbs., 1.8-kg.)
- For the rub
- ½ cup of mayonnaise
- Salt, to taste
- ¾ teaspoon of brown sugar
- ¼ cup of ground mustard
- 2 tablespoons of black pepper, to taste
- 1 teaspoon of onion powder
- 1 ½ tablespoons of ground cuminutes

- 1 ½ tablespoons of chili powder
- 2 tablespoons of cayenne pepper, to taste
- ½ tablespoon of old bay seasoning
- ½ teaspoon of the filling
- 3 cups of sliced green apples

**Directions:**

1. In a good bowl, combine the salt, brown sugar, brown mustard, black pepper, onion powder, ground cumin, chili powder, cayenne pepper, and old bay seasoning. Set aside.
2. After placing sliced green apples into the turkey's cavity, spread mayonnaise over the bird's skin.
3. When the turkey has been covered with the dry spice mixture, wrap it in aluminum foil.
4. To keep the turkey fresh, marinate it over night and store it in the refrigerator.
5. Take the turkey out of the fridge the next day and let it defrost at room temperature.
6. Spray cooking spray on the griddle's cooking surface.
7. Switch the four burners to medium-low heat and switch on the burners.
8. Let the griddle 5 minutes to heat up.
9. Smoke the turkey for four hours, or until it reaches a temperature of 170 degrees.
10. Take the griddle off the smoked turkey and serve it.
11. Serve.

# Pork Recipes

## Herb-rusted Mediterranean Pork Tenderloin

Time to prepare: 2 hours
Time to cook: 30 minutes
Servings: 4

**Ingredients:**

- 1 pound pork tenderloin
- 1 tablespoon olive oil
- 2 teaspoons dried oregano
- 3/4 teaspoon lemon pepper
- 1 teaspoon garlic powder
- 1/4 cup parmesan cheese, grated
- 3 tablespoons olive tapenade

**Directions:**

1. Lay down a large piece of plastic wrap over the meat.
2. After liberally rubbing the tenderloin with oil, season it with oregano, garlic powder, and lemon pepper.
3. Keep chilled for two hours.
4. Turn the griddle's heat up to medium-high.
5. Place the pork on a cutting board, take off the plastic wrap, and make a longitudinal incision through the tenderloin's center to flatten the meat out but not completely through it.
6. In a small mixing bowl, combine the tapenade and parmesan. Rub the mixture into the tenderloin's center and then bring the flesh back together.
7. Connect with 2-inch-diameter twine.
8. Grill the tenderloin for 20 minutes, turning it once, or until it reaches an internal temperature of 145°F.
9. Place the tenderloin on a chopping board.
10. Cover with foil and let to rest for ten minutes.

11. Slice the meat into 1/4-inch-thick slices after removing the string..

## Paprika Dijon Pork Tenderloin

Time to prepare: 10 minutes
Time to cook: 4 hours
Servings: 6
**Ingredients:**

- 2 1 lb pork tenderloins
- 2 tablespoons Dijon mustard
- 1-1/2 teaspoons smoked paprika
- 1 teaspoon salt
- 2 tablespoons olive oil

**Directions:**

1. Lay down a large piece of plastic wrap over the meat.
2. Combine the mustard and paprika in a small bowl.
3. Put the heat on your griddle to medium.
4. Evenly cover the tenderloins with the mustard mixture by rubbing it on.
5. Put the tenderloins on the Griddle and cook until the internal temperature reaches 135°F and both sides are thoroughly browned.
6. Take the tenderloins off the Griddle and let them rest for 5 minutes before cutting and serving.

## Pork Ribs with Low-Sugar Ketchup

Time to prepare: 15 minutes
Time to cook: 2 hrs
Serves: 6
**Per Serving**: Calories 392; Fat 32g; Sodium 354mg; Carbs 14g; Fiber 1.2g; Sugar 5g; Protein 31g
**Ingredients:**

- 3 pounds country-style pork ribs
- 1 cup low-sugar ketchup
- ½ cup water
- ¼ cup onion, chopped
- ¼ cup cider vinegar or wine vinegar
- ¼ cup light molasses
- 2 tablespoons worcestershire sauce
- 2 teaspoons chili powder
- 2 garlic cloves, minced

**Directions:**

1. In a saucepan, combine the ketchup, garlic, onion, vinegar, molasses, Worcestershire sauce, and water. Bring this mixture to a boil, then simmer it for 15 minutes, stirring occasionally.
3. Spray cooking spray on the griddle's cooking surface.
4. Switch the four burners to medium-low heat and turn on the burners.
5. Let the griddle 5 minutes to warm up.
6. Lay the ribs, bone-side down, on the griddle and cook for 1 1/2 to 2 hours, baste with sauce as needed.
7. Plate up and enjoy with the leftover sauce!

## Pork Chops with Pineapple and Bacon

Time to prepare: 15 minutes
Time to cook: 60 minutes
Serves: 6
**Per Serving**: Calories 339; Fat 13g; Sodium 421mg; Carbs 16g; Fiber 4.1g; Sugar 3.2g; Protein 27g

**Ingredients:**

- 1 large whole pineapple
- 6 pork chops
- 12 slices thick-cut bacon
- ¼ cup honey

- ⅛ teaspoon cayenne pepper, to taste

**Istructions:**

1. Spray cooking spray on the griddle's cooking surface.
2. Switch the four burners to medium heat and crank the knobs.
3. Let the griddle 5 minutes to heat up.
4. Cut the pineapple's top and bottom off, then peel it by slicing the skin off in sections.
5. Cut each pineapple quarter into six pieces.
6. Wrap a bacon slice around each piece of pineapple, securing it at each end with a toothpick.
7. Spread honey over the quarters and top with cayenne pepper.
8. After the bacon is done, turn the quarters over so that both sides are uniformly griddled.
9. Coat pork chops with honey and cayenne pepper and fry them while the pineapple quarters are cooking. on the griddle.
10. Cover it with foil and simmer it for 20 minutes.
11. After flipping, grill the chops for a further 10 to 20 minutes, or until done.
12. Place a quarter of pineapple on the side of each chop.

## Sausage Mixed Grill

Time to prepare: 5 minutes
Time to cook: 22 minutes
Servings: 4 slices

**Ingredients:**

- 8 mini bell peppers
- 2 heads radicchio cut into 6 wedges Canola oil, for brushing
- Sea salt
- Freshly ground black pepper
- 6 breakfast sausage links
- 6 hot or sweet Italian sausage links

**Directions:**

1. Set the Griddle to medium-high heat in step 1.

2. Apply the oil to the radicchio and bell peppers. Add salt and black pepper to taste.
3. Cook the bell peppers and radicchio for 10 minutes on the griddle.
4.  minutes pass without a flip.
5. In the meanwhile, stab or slice the sausages, then brush them with part of the oil.
6. Take out the veggies and put them aside after 10 minutes. Reduce the temperature to medium. The sausages should be placed on the griddle and cooked for 6–7 minutes.
8. After six more minutes of cooking, flip the sausages. Sausage should be taken from the griddle.


## Teriyaki-Marinated Pork Sirloin Tip Roast

Time to prepare: 45 minutes
Time to cook: 90 minutes
Servings: 4
**Ingredients:**

- 1 (1½ to 2 pounds) pork sirloin tip roast
- Teriyaki marinade, for example, Mr. Yoshida's Original Gourmet Marinade

**Directions:**
1. Use paper to dry the roast.
Spread the teriyaki marinade over the roast using a 1-gallon cooler storage bag or a container that can be sealed.
3. Medium-term refrigeration is recommended, with frequent turning.
4. Cook the beef at 180°F for 40 minutes.
5. Raise the temperature to 325°F after 40 minutes.
6. Cook the roast until it reaches an internal temperature of 145°F at its thickest point.


## Prime Rib of Pork

Time to prepare: 30 minutes
Time to cook: 3 hours
Servings: 6

**Ingredients:**

- 1 (5-pound) rack of pork, around 6 ribs
- ¼ cup roasted garlic
- Extra-virgin olive oil
- 6 tablespoons Jan's Original Dry Rub, Pork Dry Rub, or your preferred pork roast rub

**Directions:**

1. Remove the pork rack's top and silver skin. Working a spoon handle beneath the bone membrane until you can pull it off can help you remove the membrane from the bones.

2. Liberally coat the meat with olive oil on both sides. Rub the meat with the seasoning, covering all surfaces. Refrigerate the seasoned pork rack for 2 to 4 hours, or for medium-term, after double wrapping it in plastic wrap.

3. Take the marinated pork rack out of the fridge, letting it come to room temperature for 30 minutes before cooking. the griddle to 225 degrees Fahrenheit.

4. Lay the rack directly on the Griddle, rib-side down.

5. Cook the pork rack for 1 to 112 hours, or until it reaches an internal temperature of 140°F.

6. Take the meat from the Griddle and allow it to rest for 15 minutes in a free-standing foil tent before slicing.


## Florentine Ribeye Pork Loin

Time to prepare: 30 minutes
Time to cook: 70 minutes
Servings: 7

**Ingredients:**

- 1 (3-pound) boneless ribeye pork loin roast
- 4 tablespoons extra-virgin olive oil, divided

- 2 tablespoons Pork Dry Rub or your favorite pork seasoning 4 bacon slices
- 6 cups fresh spinach
- 1 small red onion, diced
- 6 cloves garlic, cut into thin slivers
- ¾ cup shredded mozzarella cheese

**Directions:**

1. Remove any excess fat and silver skin.
2. Either butterfly the pork loin yourself, or ask the butcher to do it for you.
3. There are a ton of excellent videos online that provide detailed instructions on how to use different ways for butterflying a loin roast.
4. Apply 2 tablespoons of olive oil to the butterflied roast on each side.
5. Use the rub to season the two sides.
6. On a big griddle over medium heat, cook the bacon. Set aside and disintegrate. Put the bacon grease aside.
7. Grill the pork loin for 60 to 75 minutes, or until it reaches an internal temperature of 140°F at its thickest point.
8. Against expectations, let the pork loin rest for 15 minutes in a free-standing foil tent before slicing.

# Lamb Recipes

## Grilled Lamb Burgers

Time to prepare: 10 minutes
Time to cook: 20 minutes
Servings: 5
**Ingredients:**

- 1 ¼ lb. ground lamb
- 1 egg
- 1 teaspoon. dried oregano
- 1 teaspoon. dry sherry
- 1 teaspoon. white wine vinegar
- 4 garlic cloves, minced
- Red pepper to taste
- ½ cup chopped green onions
- 1 tbsp. chopped mint
- 2 tbsp. chopped cilantro
- 2 tbsp. dry breadcrumbs
- 1/8 teaspoon. salt to taste
- ¼ teaspoon. ground black pepper
- 5 hamburger buns

**Directions:**

1. Grease the grates of a griddle and heat it to 350–450°F.
2. Combine all the ingredients listed on the list, except the buns, in a large mixing basin using clean hands.
3. Form the mixture into roughly five patties and put them aside.
4. Put the lamb patties on the prepared grill and cook for 7 to 9 minutes, flipping once, or until a thermometer inserted into the center of the meat registers 160°F.

Put the lamb patties on hamburger buns, top with your preferred toppings, and chow down.

## Lamb Shank

Time to prepare: 10 minutes
Time to cook: 4 hours
Servings: 6
**Ingredients:**

- 8-oz. red wine
- 2-oz. whiskey
- 2 tbsp. minced fresh rosemary
- 1 tbsp. minced garlic
- Black pepper to taste
- 6 (1 ¼-lb.) lamb shanks

**Ingredients:**

1. Combine all of the ingredients, except the lamb shank, well.
2. Place the marinade and lamb shank in a big resealable bag.
3. Thoroughly shake the bag after sealing it.
4. Place in the fridge for approximately 24 hours.
5. Set the griddle to 225°F for preheating.
6. Place the lamb leg on the Griddle and cook it for approximately 4 hours.

## Lamb Skewers

Time to prepare: 5 minutes
Time to cook: 10 minutes
 Servings: 6
**Ingredients:**

- 1 lemon, juiced
- 2 garlic cloves, crushed
- 2 red onions, chopped
- 1 tbsp. thyme, chopped
- Salt and pepper to taste
- 1 teaspoon. oregano
- 1/3 cup oil

- ½ teaspoon. cuminutes
- 2 lb. cubed lamb leg

**Directions:**

1. Put the chunked lamb in the fridge.
2. Combine the remaining ingredients. Including the meat.
3. Keep chilled the next day.
4. After patting the meat dry, thread it onto several wooden or metal skewers.
5. Water should be absorbed into wooden skewers.
6. Heat your griddle to 450°F while keeping the lid covered.
7. Grill for 4-6 minutes each side while covered.
8. Serve.


## Lamb Ribs Rack

Time to prepare: 10 minutes
Time to cook: 2 hours
1. Servings: 2

**Ingredients:**

- 2 tbsp. fresh sage
- 2 tbsp. fresh rosemary
- 2 tbsp. fresh thyme
- 2 peeled garlic cloves
- 1 tbsp. honey
- Black pepper to taste
- ¼ cup olive oil
- 1 (1 ½-lb.) trimmed rack lamb ribs.

**Directions:**

1. Use a blender to combine all the items.
2. Add oil gradually and pulse until a smooth paste forms.
3. Generously cover the rib rack with paste and chill for about 2 hours.
4. hours.

5. Set the griddle to 225°F for preheating.

6. Place the rib rack on the Griddle and cook for about 2 hours.

7. Take the rib rack from the griddle and place it on a cutting board. Let it sit there for 10 to 15 minutes before cutting.

8. Slice the rib rack into individual ribs of the same size using a sharp knife and serve.

## Lamb Chops

Time to prepare: 10 minutes

Time to cook: 12 minutes

Servings: 6

**Ingredients:**

- 6 (6-oz.) lamb chops
- 3 tbsp. olive oil
- Salt and ground black pepper to taste

**Directions:**

1. Set the Griddle at 450°F.

2. Oil the lamb and evenly sprinkle it with salt and black pepper.

3. Place the chops on the grill and cook them for 4-6 minutes on each side.

## Cocoa Crusted Grilled Flank Steak

Time to prepare: 15 minutes

Time to cook: 6 minutes

Servings: 7

**Ingredients:**

- 1 tbsp. cocoa powder
- 2 tbsp. chili powder
- 1 tbsp. chipotle chili powder
- ½ tbsp. garlic powder
- ½ tbsp. onion powder

- 1–1/2 tbsp. brown sugar
- 1 tbsp. cuminutes
- 1 tbsp. smoked paprika
- 1 tbsp. kosher salt
- ½ tbsp. black pepper
- 1 tbsp. olive oil
- 4 lb. Flank steak

**Directions:**

1. In a mixing bowl, stir together the cocoa, chili powder, chipotle, garlic powder, onion powder, sugar, cumin, and paprika.
2. Oil the steak and then rub both sides with the chocolate mixture.
3. With the lid covered, preheat your griddle for 15 minutes.
4. Grill the beef for 5 minutes, or until it reaches an internal temperature of 135°F.
5. To enable the fluids to redistribute, remove the meat from the grill and let it cool for 15 minutes.
6. Cut the meat on a sharp diagonal and against the grain.
7. Dish out and savor.

## Bone In-Turkey Breast

Time to prepare: 20 minutes
Time to cook: 2 hours
Servings: 7

**Ingredients:**

- 1 (8–10 lbs.) boned turkey breast
- 6 tbsp. extra-virgin olive oil
- 5 Yang original dry lab or poultry seasonings

**Directions:**

1. Set up an indirect cooking griddle and heat it to 225 degrees Fahrenheit.
2. Season the turkey with oil and set it on the griddle.

3. Smoke the deboned turkey breast for two hours at 225°F directly on a V rack or grill.

4. Increase the pit temperature to 325°F after two hours of hickory smoke.

5. Roast the turkey breast until the juices run clear and the internal temperature reaches 170°F.

6. For 20 7. minutes, place the hickory-smoked turkey breast beneath a loose foil cover before scraping the grain.

## Grilled Lamb Sandwiches

Time to prepare: 5 minutes
Time to cook: 40 minutes
Servings: 6

**Ingredients:**
- 1 (4 lbs.) boneless lamb
- 1 cup raspberry vinegar
- 2 tbsp. olive oil
- 1 tbsp. chopped fresh thyme
- 2 pressed garlic cloves
- ¼ teaspoon. salt to taste
- ¼ teaspoon. ground pepper
- 1 sliced bread

**Directions:**

1. Add the raspberry vinegar, oil, thyme, and garlic to a large mixing bowl and well stir to blend. Add the lamb, mix, and then refrigerate for at least eight hours or overnight.

2. After that, throw away the marinade and add salt and pepper to taste to the lamb. The lamb should be seasoned, added to a griddle or grill, and cooked for 30 to 40 minutes or until it reaches a temperature of 150°F.

3. Once the lamb has finished cooking, let it to cool for a few minutes before slicing and serving it on bread with your preferred garnish.

# Yan's Grilled Quarters

Time to prepare: 20 minutes
Time to cook: 90 minutes
Servings: 4

**Ingredients:**

- 4 fresh or thawed frozen chicken quarters
- 4–6 glasses extra-virgin olive
- 4 tbsp. Yang original dry lab

**Directions:**

1. Set a griddle for indirect cooking to 325 degrees Fahrenheit.
2. Season the chicken with oil and spices.
3. Grill the chicken for 1 hour at 325 degrees Fahrenheit.
4. To finish the chicken and crisp the skin, increase the pit temperature to 400°F after an hour.
5. Remove the crispy chicken from the grill when the thighs and feet achieve a temperature of 180°F and the juice becomes clear.
6. Let the crispy grilled chicken to cool for 15 minutes beneath a loose foil tent before eating.

# Fish and Seafood Recipes

## Cajun Smoked Catfish

Time to prepare: 15 minutes
Time to cook: 2 hours
Servings: 4
**Ingredients:**
- 4 catfish fillets (5 oz each)
- ½ cup Cajun seasoning
- 1 teaspoon ground black pepper
- 1 tbsp smoked paprika
- ¼ teaspoon cayenne pepper
- 1 teaspoon hot sauce
- 1 teaspoon granulated garlic
- 1 teaspoon onion powder
- 1 teaspoon thyme & 1 teaspoon salt or more to taste 2 tbsp chopped fresh parsley

**Directions:**
1. Fill the bottom of a square or rectangular dish with water. Add 4 tbsp of salt. Put the catfish fillets in the serving plate. For 3 to 4 hours, refrigerate the dish covered.
2. In a mixing bowl, combine the paprika, cayenne, spicy sauce, onion, salt, thyme, garlic, and Cajun spice.
3. Take the fish out of the dish and set it aside until it reaches room temperature, perhaps a few minutes. Using a paper towel, dry the fish.
4. Generously rub the spice mixture into each fillet.
5. To start the fire, turn the griddle on smoke and leave the lid open for 5 minutes.
6. Maintain lid closed and raise temperature to 200°F.
7. Spread the fish fillets out on the griddle grate, then cover it.
8. Cook the fish for about two hours, or until it is flaky.

9. Take the fillets from the griddle and set them aside to cool for a while.

10. Serve with freshly cut parsley as a garnish.

## Crab stuffed Lingcod

Time to prepare: 20 minutes
Time to cook: 30 minutes
Servings: 6
**Ingredients:**
Lemon cream sauce:
- 4 garlic cloves
- 1 shallot
- 1 leek
- 2 tbsp olive oil
- 1 tbsp salt
- ¼ tbsp black pepper
- 3 tbsp butter
- ¼ cup white wine
- 1 cup whipping cream
- 2 tbsp lemon juice
- 1 tbsp lemon zest

Crab mix:
- 1 lb. crab meat
- ⅓ cup mayo
- ⅓ cup sour cream
- ⅓ cup lemon cream sauce
- ¼ green onion, chopped
- ¼ tbsp black pepper
- ½ tbsp old bay seasoning

Fish:
- 2 lb. lingcod
- 1 tbsp olive oil

- 1 tbsp salt
- 1 tbsp paprika
- 1 tbsp green onion, chopped
- 1 tbsp Italian parsley

**Directions:**

Lemon cream sauce:

1. Finely chop the leeks, garlic, and shallot and add them to a skillet with the butter, oil, salt, and pepper.
2. On a medium-hot pan, sauté.
3. Add whipping cream after white wine is used to deglaze. The sauce should be heated to a boil before being simmered for three minutes.
4. Add lemon zest and juice. Smoothly blend the sauce.
5. Save 1/3 cup for the crab mixture.

Crab mix:

1. Place all the ingredients in a mixing dish and stir vigorously to incorporate.
2. Organize

Fish:

1. Slice the salmon into 6-oz parts, then heat your Griddle to high heat.
2. Turn the fish over on a cutting board and cut it in half across the center, leaving a half-inch border on either end for a lovely pouch.
3. After applying oil to the fish, arrange them on a baking pan. Sprinkle salt on top.
4. Fill each fish with crab mixture, top with paprika, and cook on the griddle.
5. If the fillets are more than 2 inches thick, cook for 15 minutes or longer.
6. Take the fish out of the water and place them on serving dishes. Spoon the remaining lemon cream sauce on each fish and decorate with onions and parsley.

## Salmon Fillets with Basil Butter e Broccolini

Time to prepare: 10 minutes
Time to cook: 12 minutes
Servings: 2

**Ingredients:**

- 2 (6-oz) salmon fillets, skin removed
- 2 tbsp butter, unsalted
- 2 basil leaves, minced
- 1 garlic clove, minced
- 6 oz broccolini
- 2 teaspoon olive oil
- Sea salt, to taste

**Directions:**

1. Butter, garlic, and basil must be completely mixed. Form into a ball and refrigerate until ready to serve.
2. Turn the griddle's heat up to medium-high.
3. Add salt to the fish fillet.
4. In a bowl, combine the broccolini, salt, and olive oil. Toss to combine, then put aside.
5. Cook salmon on a griddle for 12 minutes with the skin side down. 4 minutes after turning on the stove, add the fish.
6. Let it rest while the broccolini is cooking.
7. Add the broccolini to the Griddle and cook for approximately 6 minutes, tossing the vegetables regularly.
8. Serve with a side of broccolini and top each salmon fillet with a piece of basil butter.


## Spiced Snapper with Mango and Red Onion Salad

Time to prepare: 10 minutes
Time to cook: 20 minutes
Servings: 4

**Ingredients:**

- 2 red snappers, cleaned
- Sea salt
- ⅓ cup tandoori spice
- Olive oil, plus more for Griddle
- Extra-virgin olive oil, for drizzling
- Lime wedges, for serving

For the salsa:
- 1 ripe of firm mango, peeled and chopped
- 1 small red onion, thinly sliced
- 1 bunch of cilantro, coarsely chopped
- 3 tbsp fresh lime juice

**Directions:**

1. Mango, onion, cilantro, lime juice, and a good pinch of salt should all be combined. Add more olive oil and give it another spin to coat.
2. Lay the snapper out on a cutting board and use paper towels to pat it dry. Every 2" on both sides, make transverse, diagonal cuts along the body that reach all the way to the bones.
3. Salt the fish both inside and out. Apply tandoori spice on fish.
4. Brush oil on the griddle and heat it to a medium-high temperature.
5. Grill the fish for 10 minutes, stirring occasionally, or until the skin is puffy and browned.
6. Turn the fish over and griddle it for 8 to 12 minutes, or until the skin is puffy and faintly browned on the other side.
7. Place on a plate.
8. Garnish each serving with a mango salad and a slice of lime.


## Glazed Salmon

Time to prepare: 15 minutes
Time to cook: 36 minutes
Servings: 4
**Ingredients:**

- 1/3 cup low-sodium soy sauce
- 1/3 cup fresh orange juice
- ¼ cup maple syrup
- 1 scallion, chopped
- 1 teaspoon garlic powder
- 1 teaspoon ground ginger
- 1 (1½ pound) salmon fillet

**Directions:**

For marinade:

1. Combine all the ingredients in a dish, except the salmon.
2. Combine fish with 2/3 cup of the marinade in a small bowl.
3. Marinate in the refrigerator for approximately an hour, turning periodically.
4. Save aside the leftover marinade.
5. Turn the outside gas griddle's heat to medium.
6. Grease the pan.
7. Put the skin-side-down salmon fillets on the griddle and cover with the cooking dome.
8. Cook for 15 to 18 minutes on each side.
9. Apply the saved marinade to the salmon fillet during the last five minutes of cooking.
10. Take the salmon fillet out of the pan and set it on a chopping board.
11. Fillet the fish to your preferred size, then plate.

## Sweet e Sour Salmon

Time to prepare: 15 minutes
Time to cook: 38 minutes
Servings: 4

**Ingredients:**

- 4 teaspoons olive oil, divided
- ¼ cup dark brown sugar

- ¼ cup pineapple juice
- 2 tablespoons fresh lemon juice
- 2 tablespoons white vinegar
- ½ teaspoon paprika
- ½ teaspoon cayenne pepper
- ¼ teaspoon garlic powder
- Salt and ground black pepper, as required
- 4 (5-ounce) salmon fillets

**Directions:**

1. Combine the other ingredients in a skillet with 2 tablespoons of oil, except the salmon fillets.
2. Over low heat, stir periodically until the oil mixture is brought to a boil in the saucepan.
3. Lower the heat to low, cover the pan, and simmer for 15 minutes.
4. minutes, occasionally stirring.
5. Turn the outside gas griddle's heat to medium.
6. Grease the pan.
7. Sprinkle salt and black pepper over the salmon fillets after rubbing with the remaining olive oil.
8. Cook the salmon fillets on the griddle for 3 to 4 minutes on each side.
9. Take the salmon fillets from the griddle and brush the honey sauce on each fillet.
10. Present hot.


## Cod Parcel

Time to prepare: 10 minutes
Time to cook: 24 minutes
Servings: 4)

**Ingredients:**

- 4 (4-ounce) cod fillets
- ¼ cup fresh lemon juice

- 2 tablespoons coconut oil, melted
- 2 tablespoons fresh rosemary, chopped
- Salt and ground black pepper, as required 1 onion, slice thinly

**Directions:**

1. Turn the outside gas griddle's heat up to medium-high.
2. Place four foil squares in a square pattern on a flat surface.
3. Top each square of foil with one fish fillet.
4. Combine the lemon juice, coconut oil, rosemary, salt, and pepper in a bowl.
5. Sprinkle fish fillets equally with the parsley mixture.
6. Place onion slices.
7. To seal the cod mixture, fold the foil over it.
8. Put the cod portions on the griddle and fry them for approximately 5-7 minutes on each side.

## Spiced Whole Trout

Time to prepare: 10 minutes
Time to cook: 20 minutes
Servings: 2

**Ingredients:**

- 1 teaspoon vegetable oil
- 2 teaspoons fresh lemon juice
- 1 teaspoon ground cuminutes
- 1 teaspoon spicy Hungarian paprika
- 1 teaspoon red chili powder
- Salt and ground black pepper, as required 1 whole trout, cleaned

**Directions:**

1. Turn the outside gas griddle's heat up to medium-high.
2. Combine the oil, the additional ingredients, and the fish in a dish.
3. Cut the fish deeply on each side with a knife.
4. Liberally rub the spice mixture into the fish.

5. Put the fish on a plate and put it in the fridge for at least an hour to marinate.
6. Grease the pan.
7. Put the fish on the griddle and cook it for about 5 minutes on each side.
8. Present heat.

## Simple Haddock

Time to prepare: 10 minutes
Time to cook: 5 minutes
Servings: 4
**Ingredients:**
- 4 (4-ounce) haddock fillets
- Salt and ground black pepper, as required

**Directions:**
1. Turn the outside gas griddle's heat to medium.
2. Grease the pan.
3. Liberally season the haddock fillets with salt and black pepper.
4. Haddock fillets should be placed on the griddle and cooked for 4-5 minutes, turning once.
6. Present hot.

## Tuna Skewers

Time to prepare: 15 minutes
Time to cook: 5 minutes
Servings: 2
**Ingredients:**
- ¾ ounce sesame oil
- 8 ounces fresh tuna steak, cut into 1-inch cubes
- 3-4 ounces teriyaki sauce
- ½ tablespoons ginger garlic paste

- 1 tablespoon fresh lemon juice

**Directions:**

1. Turn the outside gas grill's heat up high.
2. Combine all the ingredients in a bowl, except the tuna steak.
3. Marinate tuna in this mixture for approximately 1 hour.
4. Thread the skewers with tuna chunks.
5. Put the tuna skewers on the griddle and cook for 4–6 minutes, turning once or twice.
7. Present hot.

## Crusted Scallops

Time to prepare: 15 minutes
Time to cook: 10 minutes
Servings: 4

**Ingredients:**

- ½ cup olive oil
- ¼ cup Parmesan cheese, shredded
- ½ cup fine Italian breadcrumbs
- ½ teaspoon garlic salt
- 1 teaspoon dried parsley, crushed ½ teaspoon ground black pepper
- 16 large sea scallops

**Directions:**

1. Put oil in a small dish.
2. Combine cheese, bread crumbs, garlic salt, parsley, and black pepper in a separate shallow dish.
3. Roll the scallops equally in the cheese mixture after dipping them in oil.
4. Place the scallops in a single layer on a big platter.
5. Let the food chill for at least 30 minutes.
6. Turn the outside gas griddle's heat up to medium-high.
7. Grease the pan.
8. Spread oil evenly over the scallops.

9. Put the scallops on the griddle and cook them for approximately 5 minutes on each side, or until they are cooked to your preference.

## Shrimp Kabobs

**Time to prepare:** 15 minutes
**Time to cook:** 6 minutes
**Servings:** 3
**Ingredients:**
- 2 garlic cloves, minced
- 3 tablespoons fresh lemon juice
- 1 tablespoon Dijon mustard
- 1 tablespoon agave nectar
- 1 tablespoon low-sodium soy sauce
- 2 teaspoons curry paste
- 1 pound medium shrimp, peeled and deveined

**Directions:**
1. Combine all of the ingredients in a bowl, except the shrimp, with the garlic.
2. Add the shrimp and liberally coat with marinade.
3. Cover the shrimp mixture dish and place it in the refrigerator to marinate for around an hour.
4. Turn up the heat on the outside gas griddle.
5. Place the shrimp on wooden skewers that have been pre-soaked.
6. Grease the pan.
7. Place the shrimp skewers on the griddle and cook for 3 to 8 minutes each side, baste with marinade as needed.
9. Present heat.

# Dessert Recipes

## Yummy Apple Pie on the Griddle with Cinnamon

Time to prepare: 15 minutes
Time to cook: 30 minutes
Servings: 6
**Ingredients:**

- ¼ cup of Sugar
- 4 Apples, sliced
- 1 tablespoon of Cornstarch
- 1 teaspoon Cinnamon, ground
- 1 Pie Crust, refrigerated, soften in according to the directions on the box
- ½ cup of Peach preserves

**Directions:**

1. With the lid covered, preheat the griddle to 375°F. Combine the apples, cinnamon, cornstarch, and sugar in a bowl. Set aside. In a pie pan, put the piecrust. Place the apples on top of the preserves. Gently fold the crust.
3. To prevent brilliancing or baking the pie directly on the flame, place a pan on the griddle (upside-down). Cook for 30 to 40 minutes. After finishing, depart to rest.
4. Dish out and savor

## Simple Coconut

Time to prepare: 15 minutes
Time to cook: 30 minutes
Servings: 6
**Ingredients:**

- 4 eggs
- 1 cup Cane Sugar

- ¾ cup of Coconut oil
- 4 ounces chocolate, chopped
- ½ teaspoon of Sea salt
- ¼ cup cocoa powder, unsweetened
- ½ cup flour
- 4 ounces Chocolate chips
- 1 teaspoon of Vanilla

**Directions:**

1. With the lid closed, preheat the griddle to 350°F. Next, take a baking pan (9x9), butter it, and cover the bottom with parchment paper.

2. Combine the flour, cocoa powder, and salt in a bowl. Melt the coconut oil and chopped chocolate in a double boiler or microwave oven while stirring and setting aside.

3. After letting it cool a little, add the sugar, vanilla, and eggs. Whisk to blend.

4. Add the chocolate chips to the flour. Put the pan with the mixture on the grate. For 20 minutes, bake. Bake brownies for an additional 5 to 10 minutes if you want them drier. Cut them when they have cooled. Serve the brownies cut into squares.


## Vanilla Bacon Chocolate Chip Cookies

Time to prepare: 30 minutes
Time to cook: 30 minutes
Servings: 6

**Ingredients:**

- 8 slices cooked and crumbled bacon
- 2 ½ teaspoons apple cider vinegar
- 1 teaspoon vanilla
- 2 cups semisweet chocolate chips
- 2 room temp eggs
- 1 ½ teaspoon baking soda

- 1 cup granulated sugar
- ½ teaspoon salt
- 2 ¾ cup all-purpose flour
- 1 cup light brown sugar
- 1 ½ stick softened butter

**Directions:**

1. Combine flour, baking soda, salt, and mix butter and sugar together.
2. Decrease the pace. The eggs, vinegar, and vanilla should be added. Turn the heat to low and gradually stir in the flour mixture, bacon, and chocolate chips.
3. With the lid closed, preheat your griddle to 375°F. Line a baking sheet with parchment paper and drop a teaspoon of cookie dough onto the prepared baking sheet. They should be cooked on the Griddle covered for about 12 minutes, or until browned.

## Walnut Chocolate Chip Cookies

Time to prepare: 30 minutes
Time to cook: 30 minutes
Servings: 8

**Ingredients:**

- 1 ½ cup chopped walnuts
- 1 teaspoon vanilla
- 2 cup chocolate chips
- 1 teaspoon baking soda
- 2 ½ cup plain flour
- ½ teaspoon salt
- 1 ½ stick softened butter
- 2 eggs
- 1 cup brown sugar
- ½ cup sugar

**Directions:**

1. After preheating the griddle to 350°F with the lid covered, combine the flour, baking soda, and salt. Brown sugar, sugar, and butter are blended. Add the vanilla and eggs and stir until combined.
2. Continue beating while gradually incorporating the flour. The chocolate chips and walnuts should be added after all the flour has been mixed. Add to batter by folding with a spoon.
3. Lay a sheet of aluminum foil on the griddle. Put a tablespoon of in a piece of aluminum foil.
4. Bake the dough for 17 minutes.

## Cinnamon Apple Cobbler

Time to prepare: 30 minutes
Time to cook: 70 minutes
Servings: 8
**Ingredients:**
- 8 Granny Smith apples
- 1 cup sugar
- 1 stick melted butter
- 1 teaspoon cinnamon
- Pinch salt
- ½ cup brown sugar
- 2 eggs
- 2 teaspoons baking powder
- 2 cup plain flour
- 1 ½ cup sugar

**Directions:**
Pare and cut apples into quarters; add to a basin. Add one cup of sugar and the cinnamon. After thoroughly coating it, let it an hour to set. Close the cover and cook the griddle until it reaches 350 degrees.
3. Combine the flour, eggs, brown sugar, sugar, and baking powder in a big basin. Mix until crumbs form.

4. Insert apples onto the rack. Place the dish on the griddle, sprinkle the crumble mixture on top, and drizzle with melted butter. Cook for 50 minutes.

## Bananas in Caramel Sauce

Time to prepare: 15 minutes
Time to cook: 15 minutes
Servings: 4

**Ingredients:**

- ⅓ cup chopped pecans
- ½ cup sweetened condensed milk
- 4 slightly green bananas
- ½ cup brown sugar
- 2 tablespoons corn syrup
- ½ cup butter

**Directions:**

1. Heat your griddle to 350 degrees Fahrenheit with the cover closed. Meanwhile, combine the milk, corn syrup, butter, and brown sugar in a large pot and bring to a boil. The mixture is simmered over low heat for five minutes. Often stir.
2. Put the bananas on the griddle with the skins still on, and cook them there for five minutes. After five more minutes, flip the food over. Peels might crack and be black.
3. Set on a serving plate. Cut the bananas' ends off, then split the skin in half. Remove the banana skin before adding caramel on top. Add some chopped pecans.

## Ice Cream Bread with Chocolate Chips

Time to prepare: 10 minutes
Time to cook: 60 minutes
Servings: 6

**Ingredients:**
- 1 ½ quart full-fat butter pecan ice cream, softened 1 teaspoon salt
- 2 cups semisweet chocolate chips
- 1 cup sugar
- 1 stick melted butter
- Butter, for greasing
- 4 cups self-rising flour

**Directions:**

1. With the cover closed, preheat your griddle to 350°F. Next, use an electric mixer on medium speed to combine the salt, sugar, flour, and ice cream for two minutes.

2. Spray a pan with cooking spray and add the chocolate chips while the mixer is still running, mixing until combined. If you decide to use a solid pan, it will take too long for the middle to cook.

3. A tube or Bundt pan works well in this situation. The cake should be placed on the Griddle, covered, and smoked for 50 to an hour after the batter has been added to the prepared pan.

4. A toothpick should have no trace of food. 4. Remove the griddle from the pan. Cool the bread for 10 and a half minutes. Carefully remove the bread from the pan and then sprinkle some melted butter over it.


## Mint Julep Peaches

Time to prepare: 10 minutes
Time to cook: 10 minutes
Servings: 4

**Ingredients:**
- ½ cup of shortening
- 2 cups of packed dark brown sugar
- 4 ripe peaches
- 2 cups of vanilla bean ice cream

- ½ cup of Kentucky Bourbon
- 4 stems separated sprigs mint

**Directions:**

1. Set your Blackstone griddle to medium-high heat and put the bourbon, brown sugar, and mint stems in a small pot on the griddle. The sauce needs five minutes to reduce.

2. Halve the peaches after removing the stones; then, evenly spread shortening over the meat. With the shortening side down and covered with foil, peaches should cook for about 2 minutes.

3. Drizzle glaze over the peaches, flesh side up, and rotate them 180 degrees before cooking them for another 2 minutes covered. Serve topped with ice cream and mint leaves.


## Watermelon with yogurt

Time to prepare: 10 minutes
Time to cook: 10 minutes
Servings: 6

**Ingredients:**

- 1 tablespoon of white wine vinegar
- 1 cup of plain Greek yogurt
- 1/4 cup of small mint leaves
- 2 tablespoons of lemon juice
- 1 tablespoon of e.v. olive oil, plus more for the drizzling Sea salt for seasoning
- 1 teaspoon of coarsely chopped thyme
- Honey, for drizzling
- Twelve 3-inch-long triangles of the seedless red watermelon, around 1-
- inch thick

**Directions:**

1. While your Blackstone griddle is heating up, combine the yogurt, thyme, lemon juice, vinegar, and 1 tablespoon of olive oil in a small mixing bowl.

2. Salt and sprinkle olive oil over the watermelon triangles, then fry for about a minute on each side, or until charred. Transfer to plates.

3. To serve, top the watermelon with mint and honey and season with black pepper and a dollop of yogurt sauce.

## Pound Cake with Sour Cherry Syrup

Time to prepare: 10 minutes
Time to cook: 20 minutes
Servings: 12

**Ingredients:**

- 4 tablespoons of sea salt
- ½ teaspoon of fresh lemon juice
- 1 ⅓ lbs. of fresh cherries
- 2 tablespoons of brown sugar, packed
- ¾ cup of sugar
- 1 cup of sour cream
- 1 pound of cake, cut into 8 slices

**Directions:**

1. Set your Blackstone griddle to a medium heat and bring the cherries, sugar, 1/4 cup of water, and salt to a boil in a medium-sized saucepan on the griddle. For about 10 minutes, cook while stirring occasionally, until a syrup forms.

2. Permit cooling.

3. Combine sour cream, brown sugar, and lemon juice in a small mixing dish; refrigerate until ready to serve. Cook the pound cake on the griddle for about a minute on each side. Each piece of pound cake should have a dollop of the sour cream mixture and 1/3 cup of cherry syrup.

## Seasonal Fruit with Gelato

Time to prepare: 5 minutes
Time to cook: 10 minutes
Servings: 2

**Ingredients:**

- 1/4 cup of honey
- 3 tablespoons of turbinado sugar
- Your preferred gelato for serving
- 2 whole seasonal fruits: apricots, plums or peaches

**Directions:**

1. Before cooking, preheat your Blackstone griddle to 400°F and cover for about 15 minutes. Next, peel and quarter each apple. The cutting edge should be drizzled with honey, and sugar should be sprinkled on top.
2. On the griddle, cook the fruit with the trim side down until browned.
3. Take the fruits off the Griddle and serve them straight away with a scoop of gelato. Add a honey drizzle, if desired. Enjoy!


## Griddled Strawberry e Pineapple

Time to prepare: 15 minutes
Time to cook: 10 minutes
Servings: 8

**Ingredients:**

- 2 cups pineapple, cut into 1-inch chunks
- 2 cups fresh strawberries, hulled
- Olive oil cooking spray
- 2 tablespoons maple syrup

**Directions:**

1. Turn the outside gas griddle's heat down to medium.
2. Thread the pre-soaked wooden skewer with the fruit pieces.
3. After applying frying spray and maple syrup on the skewers.

4. Lightly grease the griddle.
5. Place the fruit skewers on the Griddle and cook for approximately 10 minutes, turning them over halfway through.
7. Serve right away.

## Cream Cheese e Jam Stuffed

Time to prepare: 10 minutes
Time to cook: 6 minutes
Servings: 4

**Ingredients:**

- 8 bread slices
- ½ cup cream cheese, softened
- 4 tablespoons raspberry jam
- 4 eggs
- 4 tablespoons butter

**Directions:**

1. Turn the outside gas griddle's heat to medium.
2. Place two pieces of bread on a dish.
3. Cover one piece of bread with two teaspoons of cream cheese.
4. Place one tablespoon of jam on the additional slice.
5. Cover the cream cheese with the jam side down.
6. Continue on by applying cream cheese and jam to the remaining pieces.
7. Beat the eggs in a plate that is shallow.
8. Evenly dip sandwiches into beaten eggs on both sides.
9. Lightly grease the griddle.
10. Put the sandwiches on the griddle and cook them for approximately 3 minutes on each side, or until golden brown.
11. Split each sandwich in half and serve warm.

## Chocolate-Stuffed French Toast

Time to prepare: 10 minutes
Time to cook: 6 minutes

Servings: 12
**Ingredients:**
- 1 cup whole milk
- 3 large eggs
- 1 teaspoon sugar
- 1 teaspoon vanilla extract
- Pinch of salt
- 12 bread slices
- 3 (1½-ounce) chocolate bars, halved

**Directions:**
1. Turn the outside gas griddle's heat to medium.
2. Combine the milk, eggs, sugar, salt, and vanilla essence in a bowl.
3. Distribute 1 piece of chocolate over 6 pieces of bread.
4. Top with the rest of the bread pieces.
5. Evenly dip sandwiches into beaten eggs on both sides.
6. Lightly grease the griddle.
7. Arrange the sandwiches on the griddle and cook for 3 to 4 minutes on each side, or until golden brown.
8. Slice each sandwich in half, then warmly serve.

## Cinnamon Roll Pancakes

Time to prepare: 15 minutes
Time to cook: 5 minutes
Servings: 6)
**Ingredients:**
- 8 1 cup biscuit baking mix
- 1 egg
- ½ cup milk
- 4 tablespoons butter, melted
- 1/3 cup brown sugar
- 1½ teaspoons ground cinnamon
- 2 ounces cream cheese, softened

- 4 tablespoons butter, softened
- ¾ cup powdered sugar, divided
- ½ teaspoon vanilla extract

**Directions:**

1. Turn the outside gas griddle's heat to medium.
2. In a mixing basin, stir the biscuit baking mix, egg, and milk. Set aside.
3. To make the filling, combine the cinnamon, brown sugar, and melted butter in a bowl.
4. In a bowl, combine the softened butter and cream cheese and whisk until combined.
5. Insert the butter mixture into a bag with a very small hole. Set aside.
6. To make the glaze, combine the melted butter and cream cheese in a dish and whisk until frothy and smooth.
7. Whisk the powdered sugar and vanilla essence into the cream cheese until combined. Set aside.
8. Liberally grease the griddle.
9. Spread a thin layer of the mixture, approximately 14 cup worth, onto the griddle.
10. Go on by reusing the leftover mixture.
11. Gently swirl the filling from the piping bag onto the top of each pancake.
12. Fry each pancake for two to three minutes, or until it becomes golden.
13. Gently turn the pancakes over, then cook for another 2 minutes, or until golden brown.
14. Place the pancakes on a serving plate.
15. Glaze the dish and serve.

## Vanilla Cupcakes

Time to prepare: 20 minutes
Time to cook: 10 minutes

Servings: 24
**Ingredients:**
Cupcakes
- 1 (15¼-ounce) package yellow cake mix
- 3 large eggs
- 1 cup water
- 1/3 cup vegetable oil

Frosting
- 2 cup unsalted butter, softened
- 9 cups powdered sugar
- 2 tablespoon pure vanilla extract
- 8-10 tablespoons heavy cream

**Directions:**
1. Preheat the Outdoor Gas Griddle to low heat.
2. Line 4 (6-cup) metal cupcake pans with paper liners.
3. For cupcakes
4. In a bowl, add the cake mix, eggs, water, and oil; stir just until incorporated.
5. Fill the prepared pans with the mixture approximately two-thirds of the way.
6. Arrange the cupcake pans on the Griddle, then top with a cooking dome.
7. Bake the cupcakes for 9 to 10 minutes, or until a wooden skewer inserted in the middle of one comes out clean.
8. Take the cupcake tins off of the griddle and set them onto two wire racks to cool for around 10 minutes.
9. Gently transfer the cupcakes to wire cooling racks to finish cooling before icing.

**For frosting**
1. The softened butter should be added to a bowl and mixed with an electric mixer on medium speed until smooth and creamy.
2. Beat on medium speed while adding the powdered sugar in small batches until well mixed.
3. Add the vanilla extract and mix well.

4. Beat until smooth after gradually adding the heavy cream, 1 tablespoon at a time.
5. Decorate the cupcakes with icing and serve them.

# Conclusion

The Blackstone Outdoor Gas Griddle Cookbook is an excellent resource for anyone looking to master the art of outdoor cooking using a gas griddle. This comprehensive cookbook is packed with over 100 delicious recipes, each designed to help you make the most of your Blackstone griddle and create mouth-watering dishes that your family and friends will love.

Throughout this cookbook, you'll find a wide range of recipes that cater to different tastes and dietary preferences. From classic breakfast staples like pancakes and eggs to hearty mains like burgers and steaks, the Blackstone Outdoor Gas Griddle Cookbook has something for everyone.

One of the standout features of this cookbook is its focus on versatility. While many griddle cookbooks focus solely on breakfast or lunch items, the Blackstone Outdoor Gas Griddle Cookbook covers it all. This makes it an ideal resource for anyone looking to get the most out of their griddle, whether you're hosting a weekend brunch or cooking up a family dinner.

In addition to its wide range of recipes, the Blackstone Outdoor Gas Griddle Cookbook is also packed with helpful tips and tricks for mastering the art of griddle cooking. Whether you're a seasoned pro or just starting out, these tips can help you achieve perfect results every time.

One of the key takeaways from this cookbook is the importance of preheating your griddle. This ensures that your food cooks evenly and prevents sticking. The cookbook also includes helpful information on how to properly clean and maintain your griddle to ensure its longevity.

Another standout feature of the Blackstone Outdoor Gas Griddle Cookbook is its focus on outdoor cooking. While many cookbooks focus solely on indoor cooking, this cookbook is designed specifically for outdoor use. This means that you can enjoy the beauty of the great outdoors while still whipping up delicious meals for your family and friends.

The cookbook also includes helpful information on griddle cooking techniques, such as how to cook different types of meats and vegetables. This can be especially helpful for those who are new to griddle cooking and are looking to expand their culinary horizons.

Overall, the Blackstone Outdoor Gas Griddle Cookbook is an excellent resource for anyone looking to take their outdoor cooking to the next level. Its wide range of recipes, helpful tips, and focus on versatility make it a must-have for anyone who loves to cook and entertain outdoors.

Whether you're a seasoned griddle chef or just starting out, this cookbook is sure to inspire you to create delicious and memorable meals for your family and friends. So if you're looking to take your outdoor cooking game to the next level, be sure to pick up a copy of the Blackstone Outdoor Gas Griddle Cookbook today!

Made in United States
Troutdale, OR
07/31/2023

11687834R00064